D1520714

THE LANDSCAPE PROJECT

EDITED BY

RICHARD J. WELLER & TATUM L. HANDS

Published by Applied Research and Design Publishing, an imprint of ORO Editions.
Gordon Goff: Publisher

www.appliedresearchanddesign.com
info@appliedresearchanddesign.com

Authors: Richard J. Weller and Tatum L. Hands
Editor: Tatum L. Hands
Book Design: Elliot M. Bullen
Project Manager: Jake Anderson

10 9 8 7 6 5 4 3 2 1 First Edition

ISBN: 978-1-954081-42-0

Color Separations and Printing: ORO Group Ltd.
Printed in China.

AR+D Publishing makes a continuous effort to minimize the overall carbon footprint of
its publications. As part of this goal, AR+D, in association with Global ReLeaf, arranges to
plant trees to replace those used in the manufacturing of the paper produced for its books.
Global ReLeaf is an international campaign run by American Forests, one of the world's
oldest nonprofit conservation organizations. Global ReLeaf is American Forests' education
and action program that helps individuals, organizations, agencies, and corporations
improve the local and global environment by planting and caring for trees.

"We need a general practitioner of planetary medicine."

— James Lovelock

ACKNOWLEDGMENTS

By gathering the landscape architecture faculty at the University of Pennsylvania Weitzman School of Design and asking them to write about their current interests, this book is something of an homage to the department from which the authors are drawn and which I have been fortunate enough to chair for the last decade. That good fortune is due in part to my predecessor, James Corner, who, together with the faculty, entrusted me with the leadership of the department back in 2013. The culture of the department has always been one dedicated to critically advancing landscape architecture, not only as a virtuous profession, but as an art and a craft. Implicit in that is also belief, romantic though it may seem, that the landscape project is something potentially world changing and the essayists, each in their own distinct way, extend that tradition here.

In doing so, this book maps out the breadth and ambition of what is meant by the project of landscape architecture today. This could have been done with a symposium and a different cast of characters but, as a way of thanking my colleagues for their support and their dedication to the department, I chose instead to make a book that showcases them as a teaching team. In this sense the book could just as well have been called "The Education of a Landscape Architect" for it highlights the range that any student entering this field should navigate in order to find *their* landscape project.

I hasten to add that in addition to the faculty featured in the book, there are other faculty and many part-time instructors who have ensured, and continue to ensure, that the Department of Landscape Architecture at the Weitzman School of Design is an exceptional place to study. They include Anthony Aiello, Craig Allchin, Kira Appelhans, Javier Arpa, James Bennett, Aaron Booher, Megan Born, Alexa Bosse, Molly Bourne, Bart Brands, Ryan Buckley, Greg Burrell, Stephanie Carlisle, Ed Confair, Muhan Cui, Dilip da Cunha, Colin Curley, Karolina Czeczek, Candace Damon, Anna

Darling, Lindsay Falck, Kate Farquhar, Claire Fellman, Josh Freese, Miriam García, Oscar Grauer, Zach Hammaker, Tatum Hands, Marie Hart, Maria Villalobos Hernandez, Chieh Huang, Taran Jensvold, Nick Jabs, Anneliza Kaufer, Rebecca Klein, Agnes Ladjevardi, Trevor Lee, Kristen Loughry, Michael Luegering, Yadan Luo, Meaghan Lynch, David Maestres, Katy Martin, Anuradha Mathur, Ari Miller, Michael Miller, Karli Molter, Todd Montgomery, Misako Murata, Farre Nixon, Cora Olgyay, Laurie Olin, David Ostrich, Rachel Johnston Pires, Daniel Pittman, Yadiel Rivera-Diaz, Tess Ruswick, Abdallah Tabet, Brad Thornton, Mark Thomann, Dana Tomlin, Eduardo Santamaria, Andrew Schlatter, David Seiter, Jae Shin, Alec Spangler, Alex Stokes, Meg Studer, Jerry van Eyck, Judy Venonsky, Susan Weiler, Patty West, Barbara Wilks, Marcel Wilson Nate Wooten, and Bill Young. Behind the whole operation I especially want to acknowledge administrators Diane Pringle and Darcy Van Buskirk who ensured the department ran smoothly for the bulk of my tenure, and their successors Kristy Crocetto, Abe Roisman, Alanna Wittet, Eric Baratta, Deija Delgado, and Rebecca Jacob. I also want to thank Weitzman's former and current deans, Marilyn Jordan Taylor and Fritz Steiner, and vice dean for administration, Leslie Hurtig, who have unfailingly supported landscape architecture at Penn.

Thank you to my research assistant Elliot Bullen for his thoughtful approach to the graphic quality of this book, and to Gordon Goff and Jake Anderson at ORO Editions. Above all, I want to thank my coeditor, Dr. Tatum L. Hands, who is in fact the real editor of this book and of all the projects we work on together.

Richard J. Weller
Philadelphia, April 2022

CONTENTS

THE LANDSCAPE PROJECT

Richard Weller

The word "project"—an individual or collaborative enterprise that is carefully planned to achieve a particular aim—is clear enough, but that muddy old word "landscape" requires some clarification. For the public, landscape is probably still associated with images of countryside or national parks. But it is also possible that since images of the earth are by now familiar, many would extend their idea of landscape to the marbled swirl of the whole planet as seen from space. Certainly, this iconic view of the whole earth turned cosmology on its head and profoundly changed our worldview – signifying at once a global economy and global ecology. But if landscape is something with which we want material agency, then, as we advise our students, it is best not to start with landscape as a picture or a sphere, but rather with what is right beneath one's feet. And that there isn't much to see down there is precisely the point. One has to research and imagine the cultural and biological history of this ground. One has to be humbled, but not incapacitated by its density and its deep time. But above all, the landscape architect has then to look up and answer the question, "What now?"

In its purest sense, etched into the surface of the earth, the landscape project of designing the ground is an art of orientation. It seeks to provide forms of continuity—or, as the case may be, discontinuity—between past, present, and future and to explicitly situate the human subject within certain representations of place. However, the institutionalization of *genius loci* as the desideratum of a profession that is tangled up in the chicanery of commercial development often results in the trivialization and

misappropriation of place. It is now routine for landscape architects to claim the creation of an authentic sense of place in their designs when in fact they have often produced little more than a cartoon, and one that is easily coopted by the very forces landscape architects like to say they are resisting through their work.

When recourse to place is championed as the authentic locus of resistance it has too often simplified its subject and underestimated its opposition. Critical Regionalism,[1] in the form of the architectural or landscape architectural project, could never seriously be expected to resist industrialization, suburbanization, and globalization. What could? But what these forces of change did not factor into their planetary spree was climate change. Climate change forces the reappraisal of the values, mechanisms, and processes by which modernity prevails, which in turn leads to a reevaluation of how we use and abuse land. As the climate crisis intensifies, the subject of landscape becomes more, not less, important and landscape architects find themselves on the right side of history.

Design, however, requires more than righteousness, especially if it aspires to the status of art. The challenge for the landscape project in the age of climate change is then less one of conjuring *genius loci*, aestheticizing its palimpsest and fitting in with a given context than it is one of undoing what has been done and redirecting socio-ecological flows. This is a project of connecting the specificity of a place to the broader metabolism of what earth system scientists now refer to as the "critical zone" – the thin bandwidth of all life sandwiched between magma below and ozone above.[2]

As the inspectors of the rocks solemnly prepare to hammer in the golden spike and formally declare the self-fulfilling prophecy of the Anthropocene, all our old ideas of landscape as paradisiacal, pastoral, or even sustainable are of little comfort. In the Anthropocene all the natures of yesteryear— nature as mother or other—are replaced by the earth system as a chaotic churn of hydrosphere, geosphere, biosphere, atmosphere, and technosphere. This landscape is not a mysterious other or passive backdrop, it is a lifeline to which we cling by our fingernails.

It is no mistake, then, that the aim of the dominant design paradigm of the times—resilience—is more or less to just hang on. Defined as the ability of a system to resist external and internal disturbances without changing its basic structure, as a design paradigm, resilience salvages what it can from its more aspirational predecessor, sustainability, while giving up on its naïve ideal of a utopia of equilibrium. Instead, resilience seeks to identify which parts of coupled socio-ecological systems need to change in order to preserve the integrity of the whole. In its conservative formulation resilience teaches us to live with the symptoms of warming skies and rising oceans – to adapt rather than mitigate their root causes. More radically, resilience teaches adaption so as to buy time to work through the difficulty of mitigation, specifically time to learn how to live differently on a climate-changed earth without fossil fuels.

For the landscape project, what matters is that resilience theory moves the subject and medium of landscape from the background to the foreground. The landscape project of resilience encapsulates a paradigm shift from grey to green infrastructure, from centralized to decentralized systems, from engineering bulkheads that blithely resist change to so-called "nature-based solutions" that can absorb shock. Visually unimpressive though they may be when compared to great feats of 19th- and 20th-century engineering, nature-based solutions are more significant than they might at first appear. As signifiers of designing *with* rather than *against* nature (which not only serve specific human interests but also catalyze additional ecological processes), nature-based solutions represent a profound historical shift in how industrialized humans treat the earth and mark out their place within it.

The problem with nature-based solutions is, however, twofold: the first is semantic and the second material. Semantically, use of the word "nature" reinforces a dualistic worldview, contradicting the essential intention of the concept. It also trades on and plays into false constructs of nature as the redeemer and false images of nature as natural. The word "solution" is also problematic because it implies a quick fix, when in fact we know very little about designing ecosystems. For these reasons, nature-based solutions would be better branded as landscape-based *experiments*. Second, at the project level, the material problem is that nature-based solutions tend to underestimate the power, volatility, and scale of the very nature they seek appeasement with.

Of course, it is difficult for designers to convince their clients to undertake mere "experiments" at an impactful scale when everyone involved in the chain of command responsible for public works wants low-cost, low-risk, quick fix trophies. Be that as it may, landscape architects must take some responsibility for educating their clients and advancing projects of greater ambition. They also must take responsibility for a general lack of design experimentation in both the academy and the profession. This lack of commitment to design novelty, material exploration, and technological innovation is replaced, I think, by an emphasis on illustrating an orthodoxy of righteousness bundled under the rubrics of sustainability, resilience, and equity. Instead of these complex topics being explored through critical lenses and the art and craft of design experimentation, too often they are reduced to slogans and attached to conventional forms.

Unfortunately, this is also the case with much recent work being done in the name of the Green New Deal. Although this work represents an important triangulation of environmentalism, decarbonization, and social justice, the academics and students with whom it is popular struggle to ground their political idealism in design propositions that are commensurate with the issues they say landscape architecture must now, as a priority, engage with.

Although work done in the vein of the Green New Deal is at pains to distinguish itself from the mainstream profession (which is often naïvely and unfairly stereotyped as a sellout), the two do have something in common: both have a propensity for producing deceptively nice images of the future. Of course, design is and should be fundamentally optimistic, but this is not to be confused with fabricating false futures. On the one hand the mainstream profession continues to trade on a reactionary picturesque aesthetic of landscape as paradisiacal, and on the other the Green New Dealers tend to produce forms of soft propaganda where a switch is flicked to a post-fossil-fuel world in which diverse communities engage happily in what appears to be an almost medieval form of agrarian socialism.

Both of these fantasies appear virtuous: who could disagree with a greener, more just world? The problem is, however, that the high level of virtue is inversely proportional to the low level of design. And this is not to say paradise and utopia are not legitimate subjects; they are. It is, however, to insist that they be broached with a keener sense of history and more critical self-reflexivity so as to stay close to the complex and contradictory nature of the issues. For otherwise, as we defer to sweet nature in the case of the former and to an enlightened community in the case of the latter, in both cases landscape architects risk illustrating their own obsolescence.

This is also not to say landscape architecture hasn't achieved anything in the last 50 years or so. On the contrary, the profession has more or less mastered the craft of making relatively high-quality public space in some cities. Furthermore, projects such as Fresh Kills by Field Operations in New York, Marti Franch's Tudela-Culip restoration at Cap des Creus on the Costa Brava in Spain, Catherine Mosbach's Louvre Lens Museum Park in France, Georges Descombes's River Aire renaturation in Geneva, and larger projects such as the Emscher Landscape Park in Germany and both the Sand Motor and Room for the River in Holland, all point to expanded territory and subtle aesthetic advancements.

These exceptional works notwithstanding, it is troubling that in the half century since Ian McHarg published *Design with Nature* the profession's reach remains limited and its level of engagement with big topics such as conservation, agriculture, industry, and, though to a lesser extent, urbanization, is lacking. For example, if we were to compare the collective works of landscape architecture from 1969 to today to what has been achieved by the global conservation community over the same period, then it is impossible for landscape architecture's claims of stewardship to be taken seriously. This could, and I think probably will, change as climate change forces governments to return to spatial planning and landscape architects position themselves to take on this work.

In this regard, landscape architects need to build on, not capriciously dismiss, the ground gained by the discourse of landscape urbanism. The landscape urbanists (and here I count myself as one) not only agreed that urbanization had to be directly confronted and engaged as the dominant force of the times, they also recognized that the most important visions of a new urbanism—the Garden City, the Modern City, and Broadacre City—were at root all *landscape* visions. They recognized that if we were to envision a 21st-century form of ecological urbanism, then new forms of high-performance landscape, and not only the city block, must serve as its basis. McHarg and others had of course previously held this hope and made this argument, but the landscape urbanists sought to coopt the forces of urbanization whereas McHarg's generation tended to make plans in spite of it. More than this, landscape urbanists also realized that an ecological urbanism could not just be a question of urban form, but must also bring the city's planetary supply chains within the purview of design. In this sense the work of systematically understanding the forces of urbanization and directing them toward more socially and ecologically just ends through the agency of the landscape project has only just begun and for landscape architecture to now turn away from urbanism, as it has of late, is a mistake of historical proportion.

Landscape architects should also come at urbanization from the other side and forge stronger relationships with the institutions directly engaged in global conservation. Landscape architects can learn from and contribute to large-scale conservation projects such as the Y2Y Conservation Initiative, a 2,000-mile landscape connectivity project stretching from the Yellowstone region in the United States to the Yukon Territory in Canada; the Great Green Wall across the African Sahel; and the Gondwana Link in south-western Australia. There are hundreds of these landscape connectivity projects being undertaken worldwide today and landscape architects are rarely involved.

Closer to the scale of design as we know it, landscape architects can best turn to the way product designers and artists have of late taken to "designing with nature" but are doing so in a way that is liberated from the biological determinism this mantra has typically meant for landscape architecture since McHarg coined it in 1969.[3] In the sense that nature knows best, McHarg was of course right to urge designing *with* nature rather than *against* it, but if we take today's nature to be non-dualistic, amoral, impure, indeterminate, and, above all, technologically mediated, then today's designers in fields other than landscape architecture are taking a far more innovative approach to working with it. This means not only bio-mimicking nature's surficial forms but getting deeper into the microbiological nature of matter and its processes and connecting this to a landscape scale. It means designing *within* not just *with* nature. Nature as a thing is replaced by endosymbiosis as a process.

As opposed to just optimizing objects for mass production or crafting them from rarefied materials as signs of wealth and distinction, objects are today being prototyped as derivatives of and contributors to complicated ecological and socio-political processes over time. For example, a plastic bottle is not only a useful, cheap, and disposable thing, it is a multi-million-year event beginning in the Carboniferous and ending on the ocean floor with myriad, and mostly negative, consequences in between. If the bottle's lifecycle was factored into its design, its form and function in both the symbolic and ecological order of things would likely be different.[4] Not only that, by considering objects relationally in the larger spatiotemporal scale of the earth system the focus of design intelligence shifts from the mere proliferation of objects to the redesign of systems.

For the landscape project this approach means three things. First, by appraising a site as a frame through which to foreground relationships between where I stand and the earth system as a whole, attention shifts from the usual repertoire of place-making and programming to instead explore the possibility of different materials and processes, and different forms and symbols. Second, we can no longer just rely on the old adage that landscapes get better over time. To engage the denatured conditions of the Anthropocene requires a more deliberate attempt to connect the microbiological admixture of materials at the site-specific scale to the macro-scale of the earth system. Third, the landscape project must critically question, not automatically seek to coalesce with its cultural context as has been its *raison d'être* under the aegis of achieving a sense of place.

Heretical as it may seem, it might well be that the human subject of design, the Anthropos, needs in the first instance to be *displaced*. Of course, this broad historical and philosophical position needs in itself to be tuned to, and tempered by the specificity of any given place and squared with its ecology and the socio-political struggles of communities who are deeply embedded in places that have been betrayed by modernity. And, finally, designs should be approached as experiments in urban and social ecology that unfold and learn over time. In order to win space for greater experimentation, the norms as to what landscapes can look like and how they are expected to perform have to be challenged.

To look up from the ground and attempt to design a place should not be an act of arrogant human exceptionalism, elitism, or neocolonialism. The best design is always, to some degree, anti-design but this is also not to be confused with abandoning design. Design is a promethean gift and responsibility. If only by degree it distinguishes humans from other living things who actively shape their worlds. It further distinguishes landscape architecture from the many other denominations of the sciences and the arts that also study the landscape of contemporary culture. Together with those disciplines, we have much to learn about how urban ecosystems and the earth system can coexist. Conceptualizing and designing this symbiosis is the landscape project to which this compilation of essays by the landscape architecture faculty at the University of Pennsylvania Weitzman School of Design is directed.

1. See Kenneth Frampton, "Towards a Critical Regionalism: Six Points for an Architecture of Resistance" in L. Appignanesi (ed.), *Postmodernism* (London: Institute of Contemporary Arts, 1986).

2. For an introduction to the scientific project of the Critical Zone in relation to the National Science Foundation Critical Zone Observatories in the United States see: https://www.czen.org. For an appreciation of the way in which the scientific definition and study of the critical zone in the sciences meets with the arts and humanities see: Bruno Latour & Peter Weibel (eds), *Critical Zones: The Science and Politics of Landing on Earth* (The Center for Art and Media & MIT Press, 2020).

3. See, for example, Paola Antonelli & Ala Tannir (eds), *Broken Nature: XXIII Trienalle di Milano* (Rizzoli, 2019); Andrea Lipps, et al. (eds), *Nature: Collaborations in Design* (Cooper Hewitt, Smithsonian Design Museum, 2019); and Kathryn B. Hiesinger (ed.), *Designs for Different Futures* (Yale University Press, 2019).

4. For a fuller description of the full lifecycle of a plastic bottle see: "The Bottle as Hero" in David Farrier, Footprints: *In Search of Future Fossils* (Harper Collins, 2020), 89–115.

TIME

Sean Burkholder

Sean Burkholder is an assistant professor of landscape architecture and cofounder of the Environmental Modeling Lab at the University of Pennsylvania Weitzman School of Design. With a focus on coastal lacustrine environments, his work leverages the potentials of temporality, curiosity, and experimentation as fundamental design endeavors. Sean is cofounder of the research and design practice Proof Projects, a member of the Dredge Research Collaborative, and coauthor (with Karen Lutsky) of *Five Bay Landscapes: Curious Explorations of the Great Lakes Basin* (2022).

I n 1978 a 1,000-square-foot plot of land at the corner of LaGuardia Place and West Houston Street in Greenwich Village, New York City, was unveiled as a collection of small trees, shrubs, and grasses meant to reference the historic precolonial landscape of New York. By contemporary landscape architecture standards Alan Sonfist's Time Landscape may be a one-liner, yet its process of bringing the past into the present requires us to acknowledge that our past has not left us, but is still there, informing our experience of the present. Regarding the need for such monuments, Sonfist states, "Especially within the city, public monuments should recapture and revitalize the history of the natural environment at that location. As in war monuments that record the life and death of soldiers, the life and death of natural phenomena such as rivers, springs, and natural outcroppings need also to be remembered."[1]

Connecting our present to the past is not the only method of creative time displacement. Another strategy could be the encouraged recognition of other rates of time beyond our typical consideration. An example of this comes from the work of geologist Marcia Bjornerud, who believes that a reconnection to geologic time will "provide a lens through which we can witness time in a way that transcends the limits of our own human experience."[2] Bjornerud compels us to consider rocks as "verbs and not nouns." With our disciplinary affinity toward stones, soil, and plants, and the temporalities implicated with them, it seems clear that the subject of time is of central importance to the practice of landscape.

As John Brinckerhoff Jackson succinctly put it, "landscapes are space deliberately created to speed up or slow down the processes of nature."[3] In essence, as landscape designers, we trade in time; it is our medium. And yet, while we talk a good deal about it, seldom is time explored and expressed in constructed projects beyond a standard phasing plan.[4] Why is this? This essay will explore this question and suggest ways for moving beyond our universal conceptions of time as we work in and with the subject of landscape.

First, however, let's be clear; it is impossible to perch this essay upon the basis of a single and correct concept of time. For science, as much as art, time is something of a mystery; indeed, it is unclear if it is even real. Furthermore, as a subject of so many great thinkers, there is no way to cover the topic comprehensively. Instead, we should look to establish a position on time that positively affects how we actually think and work, without fear of having the whole concept figured out. The text that follows aims to serve as a springboard to what I would consider a temporal ethic that does not regard time as something universal and inevitable, without power or agency. Time is an ethical and aesthetic project whereby becoming attuned to multiple temporalities, design can more actively facilitate a multicultural and multispecies constituency.

The Trouble with Time

Wading through a collection of recent landscape competitions provides one with a trove of visual representations of our implicit assumptions regarding time and how it works in the landscape. Reference to blooming times, construction phasing, and hydrologic cycles are common. And while the ways of representing time graphically vary to a fascinating degree, the underlying assumptions behind the majority of this work are the same.[5] The example of a watch is helpful here. Even though watches can be designed in many shapes and sizes, most watches make general assumptions about the nature of time and how it works. Every time we design a new watch, we perpetuate the value of the time it is based upon.

In the landscape, while we believe ourselves to be designing new and novel places, if we do not creatively and critically acknowledge our wielding of time, we end up just creating the same landscape watch over and over again. Most, if not all, of the alluring charts, graphs, and diagrams used to describe time rest on the singular assumption that time is universal and experienced by all beings in the same way that we as humans experience it – effectively, they are all just different takes on the same watch.

Even if we are thinking about birds, water, and plants, we habitually slide back toward this assumption of the universality of time in the landscape.[6] This practice is understandable considering how many of us were raised under a Newtonian-inspired clock time that, to this day, still governs the vast majority of what we do. And while I have no expectations of dismantling clock time, there are benefits to challenging it and making intellectual room for alternative temporalities to self-actualize in a process similar to what author Jeremy Rifkin refers to as a "democratization of time."[7] For Rifkin, time is something worth fighting for, and the practice of landscape-making could be a formative stage for that battle.

One of the most fundamental points in this battle would be the contingency of time itself standing against the tyranny of universal clock time. Rifkin simplifies the issue down to the disconnect between "artificial" time and "ecological" time.[8] The implication here is that this disconnect and the emphasis on artificial time has separated us from the temporalities of the planet and other organisms. Our hurried paces, dictated by clocks and schedules synched to a single, universal notion of time, are entirely out of sync with the diversity of different times embedded in the natural world around us, and for that matter, within us. And while this seems like common sense, the idea that we cannot use the same meter to measure all things, this is precisely what universal time aims to do.

Many writers also describe an understanding of time within Indigenous communities to be quite different from the universal conception of it. Theoretical physicist F. David Peat's accounts of what he calls "Indian time" are reminiscent of Rifkin's "ecological time," stating that "For us, every moment is equivalent, but within Indigenous science, particular moments may have special powers or qualities."[9] In Peat's assessment, for Indigenous communities, events occur when the "time is right," not when they are scheduled. Indigenous scholar Linda Tuhiwai Smith pulls many of these ideas together as simply an issue of "distance." Smith sees our separation from the physical world and our communities—in addition to our desired control over space and time—as providing us the opportunity to operate at a distance from the universe.[10] It is also this distanced perspective that we use to establish our separated and purported objectivity when conducting research.

This subject of science and time is sticky, however. contemporary physics since before Einstein has acknowledged the contingency and relatively of time; and yet we, as clock-time people, very seldom acknowledge this relativity. In physics, it has been proven that any object's physical location, speed, and mass affect how quickly time passes for it.[11] In short, no two things share the same time. A collective "now" never exists. However, a good deal of science happens without time variables or consideration of this relativity – as do a good deal of our actions as humans. And while the implications of this relativity on the practice of science are part of a seemingly never-ending battle, the consequences for our interactions with other beings are also of concern, as we often use time as a force of subjection.

A walk through a research forest that focuses on agroforestry shows off a vast collection of arboreal experiments, many of which are motivated by growing more trees faster, as row after row is sprayed with chemicals, augmented with biochar, artificially heated or cooled, and harvested in various ways. This process is not dissimilar to other farming practices that have considerably modified the time cycles of plants to achieve desirable results through herbicide and fertilizer. Some plants, tomatoes, for example, can be genetically altered to modify their production or reception of ethylene, the gas that initiates the ripening process. In this case, plants take longer to ripen and allow more time for transport and storage before they are gassed with artificial ethylene closer to market to begin ripening for sale. In these examples, we are modifying the temporalities of these organisms for our own benefit – we are using technology as a tool to re-time or strip innate temporalities from these organisms. So what? We get fast wood and ripe tomatoes, both of which we enjoy. And while I may disagree that the worry is negligible, few folks likely care about the temporal sovereignty of a tomato or a pine tree.

However, this process of temporal modification has also been weaponized in order to control and subjugate our fellow humans. There are numerous methods of abuse associated with the stripping of time from others, incarceration being the most obvious. Still, more extreme forms include separating the subject from any form of time-reference (clocks, sunlight, media, etc.), a process considered by most as a form of torture. These more blatant acts acknowledge the power that time has on our lives (it is literally what builds them), and without it, we quickly become mindless, disconnected, and desperate.

The projection of temporalities can also be more nuanced yet still produce devastating effects. Cultural theorist Brittney Cooper says, "White people own time,"[12] and cites a litany of examples of just how this relationship between time-controlling Whites and "space-taking" Blacks has served as one of the foundational tools of white supremacy stretching from chattel slavery to contemporary urban gentrification. Versions of these same narratives are shared by Indigenous peoples across the world, many of which are also dealing with these oppressive forms of time projection. Mark Rifkin traces this history in describing the temporal "double bind" Indigenous peoples occupy "either consigned to the past or inserted into a present defined on non-native terms."[13] Rifkin argues for a temporal multiplicity that allows for the existence of native frames of reference outside of settler temporal narratives of linear progress and manifest destiny.[14]

So for us in the practice of landscape, the question remains: what can we do to address the tyrannical control and use of time? I might suggest a two-step process. The first step would be the simple acknowledgment of other temporalities and their importance with respect to how we conceptualize and understand the landscapes around us – effectively altering how we think about time. This would be understood as the development of the aforementioned temporal ethic. The second step would be the active engagement with those oppressive and subjugative forces that project dominant temporalities upon others – essentially altering how we work with time.

Development of a Temporal Ethic

A temporal ethic would, at minimum, acknowledge the existence of other temporalities occupying our lived and experienced reality. Pushing further, this ethic could not just acknowledge, but also make space for those alternative temporalities to self-actualize based on their own temporal terms, not on ours. Yes, in some cases, this simply means leaving things be, and not projecting temporal expectations upon them, whether it be under the guise of care or management or gardening. Each of these practices necessitates a type of temporal expectation be placed on the landscape, and in most cases, maintained over time – a constant reprojection of those temporal expectations.

This long-term commitment to landscape-making is something we typically applaud and strive for;[15] but understood through the lens of temporal self-determination, it becomes authoritarian and oppressive. One might argue that all participants in a landscape are too bound up in anthropological processes to deserve, or be capable of temporal sovereignty. However, this argument works to disempower and generalize the temporalities of other things, creating again one universally understood time – one that is dictated by a white Western conception of the term. The question then is how instead might we work in ways that make room for Rifkin's temporal multiplicity?

This call to action is in no way new. The French philosopher Henri Bergson offered a way out of time's tyranny through what he referred to as "intuition" to remove ourselves from our own duration and acknowledge the different temporal existence of others.[16] Following this, one can then conceive the landscape as a complex network of durations, each only partially accessible.

Theorist Sanford Kwinter defined "real" time as a "thick manifold of distinct yet integrated durations."[17] As landscape-makers, how might we develop an intuitive process to connect to, acknowledge, and foster those durations as opposed to re-timing them to match our own?

Bergson may again provide a way forward in his appreciation for films that varied film speed based on subject – something more connected to Rifkin's "ecological" time.[18] The reason this example is so helpful is that we can see how it implicates our work in landscape as we devise, choose, or co-opt tools to measure, survey, and describe landscapes and their processes. For example, the instruments and methods we use to measure geologic formations or the coastline are calibrated specifically to re-time those events into something that matters to us as humans, thus severing the connections between the event, its constituent matter, and its creative life force (what Bergson termed *élan vital*). Landscapes are forced to exist on our time, disconnected from the times that made them important or unique, and this mismatch between their time and our time has consequences.

Lastly, instead of the landscape only being understood as composed of multiple temporalities, what if landscapes also consisted of many (innumerable) such landscapes, existing in alternative and inaccessible presents? This speculation is based in quantum physics, and the concept of superposition, where quantum particles exist in multiple places in space at once until measured. If applied not just to quantum particles but to the larger world, this would be a world of infinite realities. This idea of a multiverse was catalyzed by Princeton physics student Hugh Everett, whose 1957 paper on the universal wave function speculated on the existence of not just multiple quantum states, but multiple classic states, equating to multiple observers and the worlds they occupied.[19]

Even though it was written almost 10 years before Everett published his paper, Jorge Luis Borges's 1948 short story *The Garden of Forking Paths* also explores the multiverse theory. In it, Borges describes how all possibilities could occur in different or parallel worlds. Borges's idea, or the idea of the labyrinth creator Tsui Pen in the story, was that "He believed in an infinite series of times, in a growing, dizzying net of divergent, convergent, and parallel times. This network of times which approach one another, forked, broke off, or were unaware of one another for centuries embraced all possibilities of time."[20] In this way, there was a reality somewhere where every possibility is true, but you only get to occupy one of these worlds.

The role of speculative storytelling used by Borges and others is fundamental to the practice of landscape. Much of what we do is storytelling. And methods such as "survivance storytelling"[21] (a method coined by Gerald Vizenor, that regularly mixes multiple temporalities) that build alternative narratives of hope, without forgetting the atrocities of the past, feels as genuine a task for landscape design as any I could imagine.

I understand that what I am calling for is an impossible task in practice. Like many others, my world is dictated by the clock, by my calendar, by the election cycles of officials, and by the funding patterns of federal and state agencies; stepping outside of that system of projected, linear, universal time would render my research, my practice, and to a large degree, my teaching ineffective. So instead of an absolute restructuring of time, I believe the best we can do is acknowledge our underlying assumptions and refuse to work in ignorance. While this will not fix the larger issue of temporal autocracy (something that landscape is not well positioned to do), it may generate outcomes that are more cognizant of the temporal implications of our actions, and if done properly, make space for other temporalities to self-actualize. From my perspective, this is the temporal ethic.

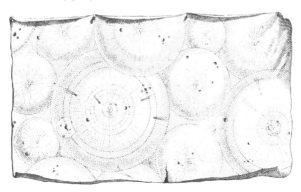

So, if we accept that our unwitting application of temporal regimes upon other places, things, people, and systems has the capacity to harm or subjugate, we must look for ways of actually working that can respond to this particular issue. Like any ethic, decisions of priorities must be made, as we can never acknowledge every temporality equally – something will always be marginalized. So how can we choose? One way forward could be through a practice motivated by the gift of time.

Landscapes of Events and the Gift of Time

In *A Landscape of Events* Paul Virilio speculates that, "Since universal world time is gearing up to outstrip the time of erstwhile localities in historical importance, it is now a matter of urgency that we reform the whole dimension of general history as so to make way for the fractal history of the limited but precisely located event."[22] In a world of temporal singularity, nothing will be more important than the spatially—and I would argue, temporally—specific. And yet for Virilio, the landscape still appears as a vessel, for events to occur *within*. Like a jar of marbles, Virilio's landscape is one *of* events. I would suggest, however, that the landscape itself is an event, or perhaps the product of many spatially specific events. This is supported by theoretical physicist Carlo Rovelli, who posits that our world is nothing more than events or relationships and that there are no "things" at all.[23] It is through these events that we actually fashion landscapes, or how, per Jackson, we "speed up or slow down the processes of nature." So, if we consider event(s) as the physical product of time, with time being the *élan vital* that powers them, our conception of the relationship between the event and landscape begins to illuminate possibilities or trajectories of engagement.

A landscape *of* events would be one understood as a spatiotemporal configuration of different relationships, containing different durations, some of which are perceivable and others that are not; and at least speculatively, these relationships are entirely different in some alternative, inaccessible present. What might thinking about landscapes in this way do for us as we attempt to establish a temporal ethic for the landscape project? For one, it clearly illuminates a context of continual flux at all scales that is rather indifferent to our actions as designers, for this process of continually fluctuating relationships does not recognize "before" or "after" design. The landscape of events is a continuum, generating novelty through the infusion of time, yet susceptible to our actions. Understanding the places we engage in this way, as having innate durations and relationships, forces us to ask ourselves with greater precision as to what should or should not be modified in a given situation. As we mess with time to achieve our desired outcomes, what re-timing is taking place and how does it affect innate durations? Could these innate durations actually become something important or foundational to the landscape?

Jackson had something to say about this idea of events as well. During his many travels, Jackson concluded that what made places special or gave them unique qualities (effectively their *genius loci*) was not the static art or architecture of the place. Instead, Jackson proposed that it is the events that occur in time that make places special.[24] Here again we see Jackson's position that it is actually *time* that makes up the landscape, and that the design process occurs through the design or interaction with events and contextual, temporal happenings that are already on the move. This is both a cautionary and exciting revelation, as there is a recognition of ongoing relationships that should be permitted to self-actualize and realization that ethical engagement within the landscape, through processes of creative evolution could generate novel outcomes.[25] For Bergson, and others that followed him, this provided a theory against the idea of the block universe, where all possible outcomes were calculable as pre-existing pieces simply reconfiguring themselves through time. For Bergson, thanks to time's indeterminacy, the new is possible and that is exciting.

But what about the temporal ethic for the landscape project? And would not any modification to a landscape require a re-timing of some innate duration(s)? Yes, this is entirely true, the temporal rescripting of landscapes is the essence of what we do; however, because of the ever-changing nature of the relational events that make up the world, doing nothing is also a deliberate and formative act.[26] Landscapes and their associated temporalities have a tendency to "fill in" the gap left by inaction, and this filling in is an example of the self-determination of local, innate temporalities. What if our primary task as designers was devising ways of making room or space for this self-actualization of events; or to put it another way, providing space for the gift of time? When asked to consider which decision to make, perhaps the option that provides the opportunity for the most extensive possible range of temporalities or the most historically suppressed ones should be our guide.

Consider the example of a forest enclosure, designed to protect plants from deer browsing. The fence provides the gift of time to the saplings within it, and it is designed for that purpose. I believe this to be one of the fundamental tasks of the landscape project – that of providing time and space through design for the self-actualization of other temporalities. This requires real design thinking, as the process of making space cannot make space for everything; thus, like any ethic, priorities must be established. Temporal autocracy manifests itself in real, physical matter, thriving through acts of classification and generalization, and thus requires real physical design to refuse or hold it back. This process of temporal acknowledgment, prioritization, and protection is not about throwing up our hands and stating that nothing can be done. It is instead about taking responsibility for what we do and owning up to the reality that we are uniquely situated between multiple temporalities and must make real decisions about how to manage the tension between them. Time is not neutral and beyond our grasp, but instead is variable, volatile, and susceptible to our actions. Working with a temporal ethic sometimes means choosing to do nothing, but more often it is about stepping up and using our influence to simply provide a landscape with the gift of time.

1. Alan Sonfist, "Natural Phenomena as Public Monuments" (1968), http://www.aldenprojects.com/2016/10/alan-sonfist-50-years-of-time-landscape.html.

2. Marcia Bjornerud, *Timefulness: How Thinking like a Geologist Can Help Save the World* (Princeton University Press, 2018), 8.

3. John Brinckerhoff Jackson, *Discovering the Vernacular Landscape* (Yale University Press, 1984), 8.

4. Although more focused on the ability to conduct time-based representation as part of the design process, Noel Van Dooren also makes this observation in "Time for Time" *LA+ Interdisciplinary Journal of Landscape Architecture*, no. 8 (2018): 37–41.

5. There are of course exceptions here, in particular, competitions focused specifically on other species such as the recent LA+ CREATURE competition, that do make an attempt to sync, or at minimum, acknowledge the temporalities of other organisms.

6. To be clear, the use of "we" in this case refers to the overwhelmingly Euro-American profession, and in particular the recent American and European competitions that were reviewed. That said, in my experience the attitudes mentioned do predominate across the world, at least within the westernized areas of the field of landscape architecture.

7. Jeremy Rifkin, *Time Wars: The Primary Conflict in Human History* (Simon & Schuster, 1989), 221–27.

8. Ibid., 236.

9. David F. Peat, *Blackfoot Physics: A Journey into the Native American Worldview* (Weiser Books, 2005), 202.

10. Linda Tuhiwai Smith, *Decolonizing Methodologies: Research and Indigenous Peoples*, 2nd ed. (Zed Books, 2012), 58.

11. A well-known example of this is the speculated Twin Paradox, where one twin stays on earth and the other flies on a light-speed rocket and after returning, discovers that time has passed more slowly for them.

12. Brittney Cooper, "The Racial Politics of Time," *TED.com* (October 2016), https://www.ted.com/talks/brittney_cooper_the_racial_politics_of_time.

13. Mark Rifkin, *Beyond Settler Time: Temporal Sovereignty and Indigenous Self-determination* (Duke University Press, 2017), viii.

14. Ibid., 4.

15. For an example of this process of "sticking with a site" and all the good it does, see Michael Van Valkenberg, "Landscapes Over Time," *Landscape Architecture Magazine* (March 2013).

16. Jonathan Jancsary, "The Future as an Undefined and Open Time: A Bergsonian Approach" *Axiomathes* 29, no. 1 (2019): 61–80, 71.

17. Sanford Kwinter, *Architectures of Time: Toward a Theory of the Event in Modernist Culture* (MIT Press, 2003), 22.

18. Jimena Canales, Albert Einstein & Henri Bergson, *The Physicist and the Philosopher: Einstein, Bergson, and the Debate That Changed Our Understanding of Time* (Princeton University Press, 2015), 299.

19. Peter Byrne, "The Many Worlds of Hugh Everett," *Scientific American* 297, no. 6 (2007): 98–105.

20. Jorge Luis Borges, Donald A. Yates & James East Irby, *Labyrinths: Selected Stories & Other Writings* (New Directions, 2007), 28.

21. Gerald Robert Vizenor (ed.), *Survivance: Narratives of Native Presence* (University of Nebraska Press, 2008), 1.

22. Paul Virilio, *A Landscape of Events. Writing Architecture* (MIT Press, 2000), ix.

23. Carlo Rovelli, *The Order of Time*, trans. Erica Segre & Simon Carnell (Riverhead Books, 2018), 95–104.

24. John Brinckerhoff Jackson, *A Sense of Place, a Sense of Time* (Yale University Press, 1994), 159–62.

25. In this case, creative evolution is the term used by Henri Bergson and explored in depth by architectural theorist Sanford Kwinter that describes the process of time leading to new and novel configurations. See Kwinter, *Architectures of Time*, 26–28.

26. Sean Burkholder, "What Not To Do: A case for designed neglect," *MONU* 14 (2011).

TRANSECT

Sarah Willig

Sarah A. (Sally) Willig is a lecturer in landscape architecture and an academic advisor and lecturer in earth and environmental science at the University of Pennsylvania. She holds an AB in geology from Princeton University and a PhD in geology from the University of Pennsylvania. Believing experience is the best teacher, she works to engage students in field study in all her courses.

A place reflects its history—climatic, geologic, and human—as well as current interactions of non-living and living factors. Unraveling the story of a place requires research and exploration of all these aspects of place. Coming to understand narratives of a place allows one to thoughtfully evaluate future scenarios. Knowledge of natural hazards such as coastal or river flooding and their projected occurrence is imperative in land-use decision-making, especially in light of climate change. Awareness of the processes shaping the patterns of ecological communities of plants and animals is important for restoration and management of degraded or eradicated systems such as dunes and wetlands. Consideration of Indigenous cultures that inhabited and may continue to be present in a place, as well as respect for their relationship to the land, is essential. Identification of the nature and extent of contaminated sites establishes the basis for appropriate remediation of land, air, and water and protection of human and wildlife health.

Experience is the best teacher. Field work involving observation, drawing, photography, and collection of qualitative or quantitative data allows for synthesis and understanding. Over the years, visiting a sequence of natural areas that are representative of regional physiographic provinces (areas of similar geology and topography) along a transect from the Atlantic Ocean in New Jersey to the Appalachian Mountains in Pennsylvania has engaged Penn landscape architecture students in learning about the regional ecology. This essay gives the reader a glimpse into a selection of these landscapes and reflects on the lessons that students learn in visiting them.

In tracing our path, we acknowledge that the land we are crossing and exploring is the ancestral and spiritual homeland of the Lenape people and we recognize their continued presence and connection to the land. Moving

through different landscapes provides a sense of scale and the relationship of features to one another, as well as the opportunity to perceive a site using all of one's senses. For many of our students, especially those coming out of high-density urban environments, the experience of walking parts of a transect from mountain to sea is revelatory.

At Island Beach State Park along the Atlantic coast in New Jersey, the juxtaposition of extensively developed land to the north of the park and minimally developed land in the park highlights the tremendous appeal of living at the Jersey Shore and the wholesale removal of habitat that often occurs with coastal development. Coastal storms, including nor'easters in the cooler months and hurricanes in the warmer months, are the most significant natural hazards. The widespread damage caused by Hurricane Sandy in the fall of 2012 illustrated the importance of dunes and salt marshes in buffering storm effects. Ongoing dune research is increasing our understanding of using nature-based solutions to protect communities. Small-scale efforts to build resilience through the use of native plants that benefit wildlife and allow for water infiltration in residential and municipal areas should be encouraged.

Wind and water shape dynamic barrier islands with longshore drift and periodic storm over-wash transporting sand lengthwise and landward, respectively. One can capture ecological diversity by moving along environmental gradients. As winds off the ocean diminish across the barrier island, sand grain size and movement, soil calcium carbonate and pH, and salt spray decrease while soil organic matter, nitrogen, and moisture increase. Plant zonation correspondingly shifts from low-growing sand-binding pioneers such as sea rocket and American beachgrass on the upper beach and primary dune to shrub thicket dominated by American holly and eastern red cedar and maritime forest supporting pitch pine and southern red oak on older dunes. Salt marsh dominated by smooth cordgrass and salt hay develops in protected areas on the bay side. Migrating and resident birds use the variety of habitats across the barrier island with shorebirds on the beach, songbirds in the thicket, and wading birds in the salt marsh. Following Hurricane Sandy, installation of snow fencing and American beachgrass planting helped restore eroded dunes. Current efforts to minimize vehicular disturbance of the upper beach in order to protect habitat for the New Jersey Endangered beach-nesting piping plover and Federally Endangered seabeach amaranth involves the use of signage and simple string and post fencing.

Kayaking down the Wading River in the Pine Barrens immerses students in a remarkable landscape underlain by quartz-rich sands and gravels that comprise the Kirkwood-Cohansey aquifer. Historically, the pitch pine forest was cleared for production of charcoal used in the smelting and forging of bog iron excavated along waterways. The forest grew back with the decline of this ecologically destructive industry in the mid-1800s. Historic threats to the vital water resource included an 1870s proposal by Joseph Wharton to divert water to Philadelphia and a 1960s proposal by the Pinelands Regional Planning Board to build a supersonic jetport and city of 250,000 people. Defeat of both proposals ultimately led to establishment of the Pinelands National Reserve in 1978. Today, the fire-adapted ecosystems of the Pine Barrens remain intact on protected lands where acidic sandy soils support pitch pine, huckleberry, and low-bush blueberry in higher, drier elevations and mucks support Atlantic white cedar, sphagnum moss, and carnivorous pitcher plant in saturated floodplains. State officials use prescribed fire to lower wildfire risk, create wildlife habitat, and reduce insects and disease. The New Jersey Conservation Foundation conducts research on intense prescribed crown fires that mimic natural wildfires at the Franklin Parker Preserve. Ongoing threats to the Pine Barrens include activities that diminish the quality and quantity of water, poaching of reptiles and amphibians, and off-road vehicular use that destroys vernal pools critical for amphibian breeding.

Nottingham County Park, in the Piedmont of Pennsylvania, shares a history of mineral extraction including mining of chromite from underground mines and placer deposits along Black Run, quarrying of feldspar for use in ceramics, and excavation of serpentine rock for building stone. Today, the park provides the best example of Mid-Atlantic serpentine barren and illustrates the effect of bedrock geology on soils and vegetation. Schist bedrock gives rise to hardwood forest dominated by oak while adjacent serpentine supports a forest dominated by pitch pine with some eastern red cedar, warm-season grasslands with scattered forbs, and gravel-forb communities hosting rare herbaceous species such as Pennsylvania Threatened round-leaved fameflower and serpentine aster. Prescribed burning, necessary for managing the plant communities harboring rare species, has not occurred in the park since a prescribed fire burned out of control in May of 2008. A recent infestation of southern pine beetle, a native species thought to be moving north in response to climate change, has decimated the extensive serpentine pitch pine forest.

Ringing Rocks County Park, in the "Triassic lowland" of the Piedmont, is the site of a fall field identification quiz on account of its diverse woody flora growing in the rich soils forming in diabase, an intrusive igneous rock that was emplaced during the rifting of Pangea. Students walk along a rocky trail and identify species including flowering dogwood, basswood, and sugar maple indicative of higher pH soils. The quiz ends at a large boulder field formed from in-situ weathering of exposed diabase into irregularly shaped pitted boulders that "ring" when struck with a hammer or other metal object. Students delight in striking the boulders and clambering over the weathered surfaces. Following a drawing session to capture the quality of the rocks as they recede into the encroaching forest of black birch, we scramble across the boulder field and downslope to a north-facing ravine. In dry weather, we walk up the layered creek bed of contact-metamorphosed shale (hornfels) and search for frogs and the occasional water snake in small pools in the fractured bedrock. The ravine ends at a moist layered vertical rock face covered with mosses, liverworts, and small ferns. Over the years, the decline and death of eastern hemlocks due to the introduced hemlock woolly adelgid has changed the ravine microclimate from shady, cool, and moist to more sunny, warm, and dry.

Over millions of years, the formation of Pangea through accretion of continents led to folding and faulting of rock layers evident in the ridge and valley of Pennsylvania. The first prominent ridge, known as Blue Mountain, is underlain by folded, resistant quartz sandstone and conglomerate and extends from northeast to southwest providing optimal conditions for fall

raptor migration due to updrafts created by northwesterly winds and thermals created by warming of southern slopes. In the early 1930s, Richard Pough brought attention to the wanton slaughter of low-flying raptors that was taking place at a prominent rocky knob through grisly photographs of hundreds of dead and dying hawks. These photos came to the attention of Rosalie Edge who took action to stop the horrendous practice by purchasing the property that eventually became Hawk Mountain Sanctuary. Since establishment of the Sanctuary in 1934, fall migration counts have tracked every bird flying over the North Lookout to create the longest running record of raptor migration in the world. Today, interns from around the world come to learn the methodology of Hawk Mountain researchers which they can apply along migration routes in their respective countries. Students hear the stories of interns at the South Lookout and then make their way over rocky terrain through mixed oak forest to the North Lookout where sharp-shinned hawks can often be seen in mid-October. In good weather, we descend to the River of Rocks, a boulder field of quartz sandstone and conglomerate rocks, and complete a final drawing. On one occasion, we were lucky to spot a family of black bears crossing the boulder field below our location. This final fall trip emphasizes the global phenomenon of bird migration that requires cooperation along migratory pathways to conserve land and provide critical stopover points for perpetuation of avian species.

A favorite spring field trip is, oddly enough, to a Superfund site. Located on the same ridge as Hawk Mountain Sanctuary, but to the east where the Lehigh River flows through the ridge, is Lehigh Gap Nature Center. The site provides access to the north slope of Blue Mountain that was immediately downwind of a zinc smelting plant that operated from 1898 to 1980 resulting in the death of the surrounding forest due to sulfur dioxide emissions and deposition of lead, zinc, and cadmium particulates. Subsequent soil erosion and cessation of regeneration led to development of a "moonscape" largely devoid of life. Hardy sassafras and sourgum continued to grow up from rootstock and an unusual herbaceous species, sandwort (*Minuartia patula*), thrived in heavily contaminated soils. In 1983, the larger area was declared a Superfund site and efforts to remediate different "operable units" began. The most recent effort to sequester the heavy metals involves amending the naturally acidic soils with lime and organic matter and planting native warm-season grasses. Students walk through the dramatic gap on an abandoned rail line to see "treated" and "untreated" areas and to catalogue the variety of woody and herbaceous species that have been planted or have naturally dispersed to the site. More recently, researchers of fires in complex terrain have conducted experimental prescribed fires to determine the safety and feasibility of this management tool on a contaminated site. As more is learned, land management approaches and goals have adapted.

In conclusion, field study of natural areas varying in climate, geology, and topography along a transect from the Atlantic Ocean to the Appalachian Mountains informs students about processes and patterns of regional landscapes. Moving through these landscapes, students observe changes in soils and plant communities along environmental gradients and search for direct and indirect evidence of wildlife and signs of natural and anthropogenic disturbance. In addition, they learn about the conservation, restoration, management, and remediation efforts encountered along the way. In the fall, students synthesize information in summary field trip reports that are compiled along with site photographs and drawings into a field guide that serves as a reference in subsequent design courses and studios allowing application of real-life experience and lessons learned. Something special happens on this transect: students learn that the land can be read as if it were an open book, and that as you start to recognize its language you can glean how it works as a whole. You see and feel how fragile and yet also how resilient it is. Above all, as our students start to wield their pens and write into it, it teaches them to be mindful of what came before them and may come after them.

ENVIRONMENT

Frederick Steiner

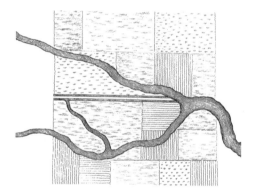

Frederick (Fritz) Steiner is dean and Paley Professor and co-executive director of the Ian L. McHarg Center for Urbanism and Ecology at the University of Pennsylvania Weitzman School of Design. He is author or editor of 21 books, including *Design with Nature Now* (2019, with Richard Weller, Karen M'Closkey, and Billy Fleming) and *Megaregions and America's Future* (2021, with Robert Yaro and Ming Zhang). Steiner is a fellow of the American Society of Landscape Architects and the American Academy in Rome.

Through a series of ordinances in the 1780s,[1] Thomas Jefferson put in place a system for settling the United States west of the Appalachian Mountains. Inspired by the European Enlightenment and classical proportions, Jefferson's geometric land-planning system consisted of a giant grid system of square miles laid out from Ohio to Minnesota. The Jeffersonian grid was later employed farther west in the United States and, after 1870, across much of the Canadian West too. Today, one can fly over North America and, looking down, see Jefferson's sweeping design. We can also see that the Jeffersonian grid had scant respect for natural features, except for the boundaries defined by the Ohio and Mississippi rivers, and the Great Lakes. The landscapes of the old Northwest Territories had been formed physically by glaciation, which resulted in rich soils and abundant water ideal for farming: agriculture was made easier by Jefferson's grid and the canals and railroads that eventually wove their ways through it.

The 19th-century explorer and geologist John Wesley Powell provided a vivid, environmentally grounded contrast to Jefferson's large-scale design for settlement. Powell was instrumental in establishing the US Geological Survey and the Ethnographic Division of the Smithsonian Institution and led the first expedition of the Colorado River through the Grand Canyon. He noted that both Native Americans and Mormons organized their communities around hydrologic systems, since water was precious in the vast arid landscapes they inhabited. As a result, he suggested that the Jeffersonian grid be abandoned and the American West be settled according to drainage basins and watersheds, raising the possibility of designing and planning regions based on their landscape conditions rather than the superimposition of abstract geometry. This essay charts the course of this line of thinking in American landscape architecture and planning.

Living in Harmony with Nature

The Transcendentalists, a group of 19th-century New England intellectuals including figures such as Ralph Waldo Emerson, Henry David Thoreau, and Margaret Fuller were of a similar persuasion to Powell. They believed that people should live in harmony with nature and this idyll inspired their works and infused American culture. Through nature, they posited, we can make meaningful connections with one another and with the world around us. The Connecticut-born Frederick Law Olmsted incorporated Transcendentalist ideas into his vision for the emergent role of the landscape architecture profession. After exploring several occupations, including farming and writing with the support of an indulgent father, the 35-year-old Olmsted began his career as a landscape architect with his design (with Calvert Vaux) for Central Park in 1857. Central Park was remarkable in many respects but often missing from discussions about its planning is the story of Seneca Village, whose mostly African American, Irish, and German immigrant residents were displaced to build the park. Homes, churches, and a school had been built in this exceptionally diverse neighborhood, taken by the city in 1853 through eminent domain. Among the many lessons we can learn from Seneca Village is that, in the United States, private property can be expropriated for the public good in exchange for just compensation. What is the public good? What is just compensation? Who suffers? Who benefits? These are questions we should ask of every landscape architectural project.

In addition to revealing racial discrimination at work, the eradication of Seneca Village illustrates that Central Park is not a remnant of protected nature but a product of design. Historically, the park area had been used for small farms, industry, and scattered settlements, and by the Lenni-Lenape before that. But the creation of an open-air refuge in a giant, crowded city proved to be an immediate success and inspired many other cities to follow suit. Olmsted, often working with his partner Calvert Vaux, an architect who had emigrated from England, designed many of these other parks, including Prospect Park in Brooklyn, as well as other visionary projects, such as Riverside, Illinois, outside of Chicago. At Riverside, Olmsted and Vaux's design worked with the site's topography and the flow of the Des Plaines River, protecting areas in the floodplain as park land and letting the natural terrain inform the road system. The resulting plan reflected their understanding of hydrology and topography. As Powell's plan for the arid regions of the American West contrasts with Jefferson's grid, the winding streets of Riverside differ from the Chicago street grid.

One project that exemplifies Olmsted's Transcendentalist ideals is Niagara Falls, which before Olmsted's design had been harnessed for industry. On visiting the Falls, he observed "mills and factories everywhere, hovels, fences and patent medicine signs."[2] Olmsted joined Emerson and Harley Darwin in the "Free Niagara" movement to remove the factories and create a park and return the falls to an "unspoiled" state.[3] They lobbied until New York Governor Grover Cleveland signed the 1883 law creating the Niagara Reserve as the first state park in the nation, followed five years later by a partner park on the Canadian side of the falls. Olmsted and Vaux's design for Niagara Falls stands as an amazing realization of reinvented nature, providing a place for visitors to "contemplate the beauty of nature."[4]

As the Transcendentalist movement continued to expand its influence in the late 19th century, the science of biology advanced in Europe and the United States. Élisée Reclus—a French geographer and anarchist—advocated the use of watershed or drainage basin planning as well as the use of the understanding of biological systems in design and planning. Reclus in turn influenced the Scottish polymath Patrick Geddes – a trained biologist and sociologist who became a town planner. In 1909, Geddes developed his valley section, a transect displaying the relationships between elevation and settlements, to help illustrate how the physical world impacts how and where we live. Geddes was drawn to Charles Darwin's theory of evolution arguing that town planning and design are instruments that we use to actively shape our evolution. He once observed, "The environment acts, through function, upon the organism and conversely, the organism acts, through function, upon the environment."[5]

Among those inspired by Geddes were Americans Benton MacKaye and Lewis Mumford. With Catherine Bauer, Clarence Stein, and others, Mumford and MacKaye were part of a small, informal group of intellectuals and architects who formed the Regional Planning Association of America. They advanced Geddes's and Olmsted's planning ideas as ways to build differently than the prevailing industrialized and crowded urban settlements in America and to preserve rural and natural areas. Asserting that regional planning is a form of applied human ecology, MacKaye conceived of the Appalachian Trail as a way to revitalize a massive region that stretched from Maine into Georgia. MacKaye also emulated Olmsted and Charles Eliot's Emerald Necklace plan to propose the Boston Bay Circuit – a contiguous metropolitan-scale open-space system.

Design with Nature

Scottish-American landscape architect Ian McHarg embraced these ideas with his advocacy of ecology and the creation of a practical method by which landscape ecology could form the foundation of modern land use planning to resist and redirect American sprawl. During the 1950s and 1960s, ecologists including Paul Sears, Eugene and Howard Odum, and Robert MacArthur were simultaneously advancing our understanding of ecosystems and community ecology. At the same time, publications such as Aldo Leopold's *A Sand County Almanac*[6] and Rachel Carson's *Silent Spring*[7] resonated beyond the scientific community as individuals like Lady Bird Johnson and Stewart Udall were bringing environmental concerns into the sphere of public policy.

Like his fellow Scot Patrick Geddes, McHarg was guided by Darwin's theories. In McHarg's case, the biologist Lawrence Henderson was a key figure. Henderson wrote: "Darwinian fitness is compounded of a mutual relationship between the organism and the environment. Of this, fitness of the environment is quite as essential a component as the fitness which arises in the process of organic evolution; and in fundamental characteristics the actual environment is the fittest possible abode of life."[8] Whereas Geddes had been interested in how people participate in our own evolution, McHarg, drawing on Henderson's writings, focused on how some environments were more fit than others.

McHarg organized the components of environment in a diagrammatic form that he called the "layer cake." Mapped information about the climate, geology, physiography, ground and surface water hydrology, soils, plants, animals, and people of a place are organized and then overlaid to determine the fitness for possible land uses. McHarg organized these natural factors in chronological order, from the oldest parts of the environment to the more ephemeral parts, that is from climate and rocks to animals and people. McHarg's layer cake helped form the theoretical basis for computer mapping called geographic information systems (GIS). He also laid the groundwork for environmental impact assessment to become standard practice.

McHarg was the longtime chair and faculty member of the University of Pennsylvania Department of Landscape Architecture and Regional Planning. He also founded the firm Wallace, McHarg, Roberts, and Todd, which today exists as WRT. With his Penn and WMRT colleagues, McHarg was engaged in many pioneering regional planning studies such as those for the Potomac and Delaware River basins, the Minneapolis/St. Paul Twin Cities, and the Colorado Front Range, always advancing the use of ecology as the basis for planning and design and engaging local scientists to ensure immediate familiarity with the study area. McHarg's ideas and method became increasingly relevant and remain so today. His 1968 study for Staten Island—published the following year in his book *Design with Nature*—is a prime example. His pre-GIS, hand-drawn maps illustrated the places that were unwise to develop for a variety of reasons, including their susceptibility to flooding from storms. In 2012, the areas on Staten Island designated unsuitable for development by McHarg were those hardest hit by the devastating Hurricane Sandy. We have the information to save lives and property, we need the wisdom to use it.

Numerous of McHarg's Penn students would go on to have influential careers in landscape architecture, architecture, and planning. Among them is Anne Winston Sprin, who had worked with McHarg at WMRT on several projects including The Woodlands in Texas and wrote the prescient 1984 book *The Granite Garden*.[9] Spirn argued that McHarg's ideas about nature and using ecology in design and planning were as applicable to urban areas as places beyond the city limits. Also in 1984, another McHarg protégé, Michael Hough, published a book with a similar theme called *City Form and Natural Process*.[10] An Edinburgh-trained architect, Hough spent most of his career in Canada. Spirn and Hough advanced McHarg's ideas about nature and design and the use of ecology in urban design. Meanwhile, firms like Andropogon and Jones & Jones continued to advance ecological design practice. At the same time that Spirn and Hough were publishing their books, Richard Forman published his important treatise on landscape ecology in 1984 with the French scientist Michel Godron. Forman had earned his PhD at Penn when Robert MacArthur was on the faculty advancing community ecology.

It was James Corner, yet another of McHarg's protégés, who started to merge urban ecology with the art of design. A teacher and theorist in his early career, Corner (with Lisa Switkin and his other Field Operations colleagues) moved dramatically into practice with the design of the High Line in New York City. The success of the High Line mirrors the earlier impact of Central Park. As with Central Park, city leaders everywhere wanted their own High Line. And as with Central Park, we should again ask: Who suffers? Who benefits? What would have happened to the lower Manhattan neighborhood without the High Line? Of Field Operations' early projects, Freshkills Park on Staten Island probably best represents and advances the design-with-nature idea. Freshkills occupies the site of one of the largest landfills in the world; Corner's plan involves stepping back from control, seeding new ecological systems, and letting nature take its course with strategic interventions along the way.

Others are also merging art and ecology, such as Susannah Drake of DLANDStudio, whose "Sponge Park" plan for the Gowanus Canal in Brooklyn is a heroic attempt to re-envision one of the most polluted sites in North America. Another is Kate Orff of SCAPE, whose successful "Oyster-tecture" proposal seeks to re-establish the oyster habitats in New York Harbor. Landscape architects are increasingly taking on tough, toxic landscapes with the vision of artists and the knowledge of scientists.

New Ecological Regionalism

Beginning in the late 20th century, several designers and planners started to advance new ideas about regionalism, often based on ecology. John Fregonese, a Portland-based planner, and Peter Calthorpe, a Berkeley-based New Urbanist architect, teamed up on several regional visioning efforts, including Envision Utah and Envision Central Texas for metropolitan Austin. Their approach used a deep GIS database of social and environmental information and charrette-based public participation to arrive at detailed alternative scenarios for the future based on transportation and land-use decisions. These scenarios ranged from "business as usual," with deleterious social, economic, and environmental consequences to much more enlightened futures based on good planning and environmental protection.

Meanwhile, Carl Steinitz of the Harvard Graduate School of Design led several alternative futures studies for the US Department of Defense. Steinitz engaged teams of planners, landscape architects, and environmental scientists in these studies. In one, he included ecologist Richard Forman for the Camp Pendleton Marine Base in Southern California. Key features of this plan involved the future of the base and its surroundings for wildlife enhancement and biodiversity. This landscape-ecology grounded approach generated several scenarios that showed how biodiversity could be expanded through careful design and planning.

A concept emerging from urban ecology, landscape ecology, and other current ecological research is ecosystem services. Ecosystem services are basically the benefits we receive from nature that we take for granted and assume to be free. Advocates of ecosystem services have identified four types. First, supporting services are necessary to produce all other ecosystem services: nutrient cycling, primary production, soil formation, and so on. Second, provisioning services describe the material or energy produced in the ecosystem, such as food, water, timber, and other resources. Third, regulating services are what ecosystems provide as regulators: regulating the air, water, and soil quality as well as providing flood and disease control. Fourth, a cultural or contributing service are those non-material benefits that are important for human culture in terms of art, religion, and recreation. Ecosystem services occur everywhere: in urban areas, in rural areas, in the suburbs, in the mountains and the plains, and everywhere in between. We should think of ecosystem services not only as an opportunity when we design and plan places but as something to reinforce into the future.

The Green New Deal

This spirit manifests itself now in the politics of the Green New Deal (GND). The GND is a clear homage to one of the most transformative, progressive eras in the history of the United States. Franklin Roosevelt led the nation out of the Great Depression through bold actions that lifted many people out of poverty and misery. The New Deal was not a single legislative or administrative action but a series of laws and associated programs that expanded the powers of government in specific ways. Sadly, not all people benefitted equally, and some groups were held back, especially Black citizens through redlining and other discriminatory measures.

The GND was introduced as a non-binding resolution on February 7, 2019, in the US House of Representatives by New York Representative Alexandria Ocasio-Cortez and in a companion resolution in the Senate by Massachusetts Senator Edward Markey. On one level, the resolution addresses the existential challenge of human-induced climate change. On another, it acknowledges the social equity consequences of environmental injustice. Ocasio-Cortez and Markey argued the nation must muster a response with the same level of urgency and resources comparable to the New Deal almost a century earlier. Transportation accounts for around 28% of the greenhouse gas production in the United States. Buildings produce another 50% and they also consume around half of the energy used in the nation. The built environment therefore presents the most significant opportunities for a greener future and megaregions in the United States contain some of the biggest cities on the planet.

If we are to reduce our carbon footprint the built environment needs to be completely rethought. We might begin by rethinking ecosystem services. Instead of depleting them and passing along polluted air, water, and soils to future generations, we should consider how to build and regenerate ecosystem services. Also, outside cities, climate reserves will benefit other species and mitigate planetary warming by serving as carbon sinks. Megaregions provide the ideal scale for planning and locating these reserves. Since it was created by Congress in 1964, the Land and Water Conservation Fund has helped to conserve thousands of acres of land across the United States. This fund should be utilized and expanded to create climate reserves.

The green thread in American literature begun by Emerson and Thoreau continues, enriched and deepened by the likes of Terry Tempest Williams, Colson Whitehead, and others. Designers and planners should continue to learn and be inspired by the close readings of our surroundings presented by such authors. One of our fundamental responsibilities as designers and planners is the protection of public health, safety, and welfare. According to the World Health Organization, health is our ability to recover from injury and insult. If we are resilient, we can be healthy.

Pope Francis's remarkable 2015 encyclical *Laudato si'* addresses the health of the planet. In the encyclical, the Pope advocated an integral ecology to bridge climate change, environmental quality, and social justice. According to Pope Francis, human ecology is inseparable from the notion of the common good as a central and unifying principle of social ethics. He urges us to design our communities, cities, and the planet more responsibly: socially and environmentally. Most of us on the planet now live in cities, so that's where the greatest challenges and opportunities arise. Over 60 years ago, in 1961, Ian McHarg declared that it was time to examine the city as an ecosystem. That message could not be more relevant today.

1. Known as the Northwest Ordinances (1784, 1785, 1787).

2. Jeff Z. Klein, "Heritage Moments; Frederick Law Olmsted and the Stroll That Saved Niagara," *WBFO.org* (August 18, 2018).

3. Ibid.

4. Ibid.

5. Patrick Geddes, *Cities in Evolution*, revised edition (Oxford University Press, 1950), 200.

6. Aldo Leopold, *A Sand County Almanac* (Oxford University Press, 1949).

7. Rachel Carson, *Silent Spring* (Houghton Mifflin, 1962).

8. Lawrence J. Henderson, "The Fitness of the Environment, *An Inquiry into the Biological Significance of the Properties of Matter*." The American Naturalist 47, no. 554 (1913): 105.

9. Anne Whiston Spirn, *The Granite Garden: Urban Nature and Human Design* (Basic Books, 1984).

10. Michael Hough, *City Form and Natural Process: Towards a New Urban Vernacular* (Van Nostrand Reinhold, 1984).

PLANTS

Sonja Dümpelmann

Sonja Dümpelmann is a landscape historian and professor at the University of Pennsylvania Weitzman School of Design. She is the author and editor of several books, including the prize-winning *Seeing Trees: A History of Street Trees in New York City and Berlin* (2019). She has served as President of the Society of Architectural Historians Landscape History Chapter and as Senior Fellow in Garden and Landscape Studies at the Dumbarton Oaks Research Library and Collection, Washington, DC.

P lants stand at the core of landscape architecture. As life-sustaining organisms, plants in their myriad forms, shapes, colors, and sizes are a fundamental component of most landscapes, regardless of how much or how little these landscapes are shaped and designed by human hands. However, as history reveals and this essay argues, plants have been both landscape architecture's strength and weakness. In the future they could be its strength. Today's concerns about global warming, climate justice, as well as social and environmental justice more generally show that it is high time for landscape architecture to reconsider its vegetal origins and the manifold values of plants. It is necessary to overcome the presumptive weaknesses that have often been associated with a preoccupation with plants.

Shedding light on plants' uses and roles in landscape architecture's history can not only enlighten the present but also suggest future possibilities of designing with and for plants. As will become clear, plants sit at the confluence of art and science, as well as culture and nature, which characterize designed landscapes. They can imbue landscapes with meaning, for good and for bad. Plants have been misused in various ways and contexts to wield power, marginalize and subdue people, and to hide them, their labor, and problems in plain sight. However, plants' changeability and malleability—that is, their "plantness," their perpetual process of becoming—also uplifts us humans. Plants' changeability has enabled them to persevere and protect us. In the Anthropocene, however, it is no longer only us who need protection to survive but the plants themselves. Through mutually beneficial collaborative projects with plants, landscape architecture is in the unique position to further understanding of the relationships between human and nonhuman nature and work against environmental crises.

Poetry

Plants encapsulate what distinguishes landscape architecture from other design disciplines dealing with the built environment. Plants are nature, both in a literal and figurative sense. They are not only a living material with their own agency, but they also symbolize nature. Plants are synecdoches of nature at large. The ways in which plants have been used and manipulated over time to create place, make space, and shape gardens and landscapes of various types has always been an indicator of our relationship with nonhuman nature at large. Plants are therefore also the subject of and the result of culture, as the terms agriculture, viticulture, arboriculture, and floriculture attest. In landscape architecture plants are both nature and culture. They sit squarely within what the early professional landscape architects described as a synthesis of agriculture, horticulture, and forestry as well as engineering and architecture.

In landscape architecture plants are more than a resource that can be harvested to provide medicine and drugs, food, and energy. They are also more than building materials and creators of space, and they provide more than what today are often called ecosystem services – the remediation of soil and water, the protection against soil erosion, the cooling of air, filtering of dust, buffering of sound, and the sequestering of carbon. Besides these functions, in landscape architecture plants are used to lift the human spirit, provide pleasure and psychological well-being, and foster identity. They are chosen and arranged for their form, sound, texture, color, smell, rhythm, and meaning. Oftentimes, landscape architecture is at its best when it employs plants to fulfill multiple of these functions and to achieve what the ancient Latin writer Horace in relation to poetry called the *dulce utili* – a mix of pleasure and utility.

This concept, in other contexts described as the combination of art and science, is one of the bedrocks of landscape architecture, cited in particular by 18th-century British landscape gardeners. It has also given rise to cultural technologies including *Vegetationstechniken*, literally "vegetation technologies," used in the shaping of the land. An ancient example is the Etruscan and then Roman planting practice of training vines on and between trees described by Pliny the Elder and other Latin writers as "married vines,"[1] and famously represented in a mural excavated in the late 19th century at Pompeii's casa dei Vettii.[2] Quite fittingly, in this ancient fresco small cupids are shown busying themselves with the vintage (while vines could be married, plane trees in Ancient Rome were considered "widowed," as they were never used as support for vines).[3] The married vine and its supporting trees were a cultural abstraction of the vines' natural forest habitat. Neoclassicism and romantic reverie turned this cultural technology into a 19th-century garden motif used, for example, in Prussia to evoke the Italian countryside. As an ongoing agroforestry practice in parts of Italy today, in some regions like Emilia Romagna and Veneto, the vines and trees—most often elms, maples, and poplars—are still planted for both utility and beauty along boundary ridges and in fields. They increase biodiversity, a concern that also lay at the heart of German forester Heinrich von Salisch's late 19th-century call for forest aesthetics. As a reaction to the monocultures of scientific forestry, forest aesthetics aspired to develop forests that yielded timber while also supporting diverse wildlife and pleasant forest scenery that fostered auditory and olfactory effects.[4] In short, von Salisch's aesthetic concerns sought to create a more robust forest ecology. Besides discussing the aesthetics of different forest plants, their combinations, and planting patterns literally creating different rhythms, von Salisch also addressed a centuries-old question: Should non-native plants be used, and if so, in what contexts and for what purposes?

Power

Plants have been used to express different aesthetic preferences and political leanings, and to foster identity. In multiple ways they are one of the "languages of landscape."[5] Not only do they respond to external conditions like climate and soil, therefore witnessing and indicating changes in the environment that they themselves also shape, but in landscape architecture they also play an iconographic role, and their species selection and use have always been political. In the United States the ailanthus, imported from China, was considered a suitable tree in urban environments in the 1840s, but in the political climate of the 1850s that was increasingly characterized by the nativist and anti-immigrant sentiment of the Know Nothing movement, opinions began to change. Many citizens began to consider the species a nuisance and public health hazard given its "oppressive," "nauseating," and "poisonous" male flower odor. Xenophobic criticism soon incriminated the imported species as a "filthy and worthless foreigner" and "fragrant stranger" that should be replaced with "hardy, sweet and indigenous" species.[6] In 1920s Rome, the Italian fascists ordered the replacement of many deciduous road-side trees with what they considered to be "more Italian" umbrella pines.[7] In Germany, landscape gardener Willy Lange gave expression to völkisch-nationalist sentiment through his early-20th-century "Nature Garden" concept (*Naturgarten*), whose naturalistic garden aesthetic was later used to bolster the Nazi's blood and soil ideology.[8]

Before the Nazis instrumentalized the Nature Garden (and native plants) for their totalitarian, discriminatory ideology and politics, it was used by German garden architects to uphold their ground in a professional battle with architects who were also engaged in garden design and strongly favored geometrical garden layouts. The only way to successfully outdo the architects, the garden architects thought, was to argue for the Nature Garden that required plant experts to design and realize it – plant experts, which *they* were, but architects were not. A similar battle regarding a similar garden concept—the "Wild Garden"—had waged in Britain.

As components of landscape designs, plants can literally and figuratively be used for cover-ups. Nineteenth-century landscape gardener John Claudius Loudon praised this "obvious, useful, and universal" capacity as one of trees' most important design uses.[9] Plants can screen, mask, veil, camouflage, and hide in plain sight not only unwanted structures or architectures but also the histories and labor that have gone into their creation. For the 18th- and 19th-century landscape gardeners it was as important to screen the various testimonies of industrial development like factories, steam engines, and coal-works as it was to hide capitalism's consequences in the form of "houses of poorer neighbors" and "workhouses, &c."[10] In the late 1980s, cultural geographer Stephen Daniels argued that "landscape… does not easily accommodate political notions of power and conflict, indeed it tends to dissolve or conceal them."[11] He encouraged the exploration of the "duplicity of landscape," of the tension that exists between an "authentic object in the world" and its "ideological mirage."[12] It is particularly the plants that can render entire landscapes duplicitous. In this sense, plants are a force, albeit in many cases a dubious one.

However, the ability of plants (and landscape more generally) to veil both cultural artifacts and their history, and to become a cultural artifact themselves through horticulture, arboriculture, and their synthesis with inert matter, has often rendered them invisible. Plants and their agency are frequently overlooked. Already in the first century CE, Pliny the Elder deplored the neglect of plants in the writings and general knowledge of his contemporaries as well as the misleading "triviality of the[ir] names."[13] During the last two decades, plant scientists and philosophers have taken the lead in describing and analyzing what scholars of education Elisabeth E. Schussler and James H. Wandersee have called "plant blindness" in large parts of Western society. This includes "the inability to recognize the importance of plants in the biosphere, and in human affairs; …the inability to appreciate [plants'] aesthetic and unique biological features…; [and] the misguided, anthropocentric ranking of plants as inferior to animals."[14] Plant scientist Francis Hallé has explained the marginalization and neglect of plants as well as the inferiority attributed to them. For example, we identify with humans and nonhuman animals that are *animate*, that are attributed with a soul, and that can move like we do. We identify less easily with plants that are immobile, voiceless, and often thought to be soulless. Throughout human culture, plants have often been associated with the "weaker" sex. Men hunted animals; women gathered plants. This power relation also becomes clear in the use of language. The word "botany" derives from the ancient Greek word *boton* describing a herd animal. The animal's fodder, plants, was *botanê*. Plants therefore are weak, and if we are "vegetating" we usually find ourselves in a weak state (although the Middle Latin *vegetabilis* means "growing" or "flourishing," and the verb *vegetare* "to animate" or "to enliven"). If in contrast we want to attribute plants with agency and strength we anthropomorphize them.[15]

However, plants are more often merely considered as backdrops and ground, not as figures or agents in history. They therefore share a fate that has befallen marginalized groups in landscape architecture. Landscape architecture's particular, yet changeable, preoccupation with plants has been part of the reason why the profession is relatively unknown in the first place, and why it has been able to attract only few people from marginalized ethnicities and has had a wavering female presence.[16] As a profession and activity that works with plants because of their beauty and utility, landscape architecture suffers the plant blindness that has beset much of Western thought and society. As philosopher Michael Marder has observed, "More often than not, we overlook trees, bushes, shrubs, and flowers in our everyday dealings, to the extent that these plants form the inconspicuous backdrop of our lives—especially within the context of 'urban landscaping'—much like the melodies and songs that unobtrusively create the desired ambience in cafes and restaurants. In this inconspicuousness, we take plants for granted, so that our practical lack of attention appropriately matches their marginalization within philosophical discourses."[17] However, through mutually beneficial collaborative projects with plants that are understood "as active, self-directed, even intelligent beings,"[18] landscape architecture is also in the unique position to further the understanding of the relationships between human and nonhuman nature and work against environmental crises. As Marder has argued, the task is to "maintain and nurture…[plants'] otherness"[19] because it is the ensuing understanding and respect for them that can avert environmental destruction and exploitation. Plants can therefore be regarded as both landscape architecture's weakness and strength.[20]

Process

One of the challenges of working with plants is their "plantness,"[21] which includes their independent life force and agency, their malleability, seasonal change, and change over time ultimately leading to their death. However, these are also plants' fundamental qualities providing creative opportunities to those working with them. Plants never cease to develop, grow, and produce new leaves, flowers, and other parts until they die. As philosopher Luce Irigaray has pointed out, plants' mode of being in the world is focused on becoming, rather than being.[22] It is focused on process and transformation. Natural transformation and the factor of time were on Frederick Law Olmsted's mind when in the early 1850s, before embarking on his own design career, he admired landscape designers' "far-reaching conception of beauty and designing-power, [that] sketches the outlines, writes the colours, and directs the shadows, of a picture so great that Nature shall be employed upon it for generations, before the work he has arranged for her shall realize his intentions!"[23] Some decades later in 1882, now as a master of picturesque and pastoral scenes within urban environments with an eye for the beauty of spontaneous plant growth, Olmsted argued that "neglect, if it continues not too long, may even have its advantages."[24] Landscape architects have repeatedly made this and similar arguments since then for various purposes. They have recognized plants' role for biodiversity, for example, and more recently they have combined this with economic arguments to improve and enhance spontaneous plant growth in cities.[25] Far from a laissez-faire approach, however, these planting concepts and designs are often highly curated. In subtle ways they seek to anticipate, encourage, and direct spontaneous plant growth, enhancing its aesthetic effects and eco-systemic benefits. Already Olmsted had, of course, stressed the necessity of plant care and management for the establishment of the aspired landscape scenery and atmospheric effects.

Perseverance

In some contexts, plants have been able to persist and persevere precisely because of their lifelong process of becoming – their inherent changeability, life cycles, and own life force. Many plants, in particular trees, outlive humans, and they therefore often provide us with a sense of permanence, durability, and stability, as well as awe and wonder. Eighteenth- and 19th-century romantic poets and painters strengthened this perception through their representations of monumental, gnarly trees, realizing that their years may be numbered given increasing urbanization and industrialization. Many foresters shared this realization, among them former Holstein forestry official Eduard Mielck. In 1863 he published a chart measuring the tallest plants against architectural monuments. Entitled "The Giants of the Plant World and the Giant Structures of the Art of Building" (*Die Riesen der Pflanzenwelt und die Riesengebilde der Baukunst*), Mielck juxtaposed a giant sequoia with the Cheops pyramid, and the famous Teneriffa dragon tree described by Alexander v. Humboldt with the obelisk standing on Rome's piazza di San Giovanni in Laterano. Among the foregrounded plants in this drawing were a eucalyptus tree, an oak tree, a hoop pine, a Douglas and a common fir, a wax palm, the famous Sydney fig tree (known as Port Jackson fig), and the still-existing Hundred-Horse Chestnut near Mount Etna. The plants were set against a backdrop created by the outlines of the largest contemporary architectural monuments. These included the cupolas of St. Peter's in Rome and St. Paul's in London; the steeples of Europe's major cathedrals; the Torre degli Asinelli in Bologna, the Luxor Obelisk in Paris, and Hamburg's water tower. To add human proportions, Mielck complemented his chart with a human figure, an elephant, and a whale in a tank.[26] However, as important as the comparison of horizontal, circumferential, and especially vertical dimensions, was Mielck's collection of tree life spans – the fourth dimension. It ranged from what at the time was thought to be 300 years for north German pine trees to 5,150 years for Senegalese baobabs that already in the previous century had been ranked as among the oldest living plants on earth.[27] Witnessing increasing encroachments upon the world's arboreal heritage in the middle of the 19th century, Mielck warned of the ensuing loss of natural and cultural heritage and of the sense of history.

Ligneous plant life is inextricably linked with human culture and history through the ideas of dwelling and building that are connected to plants' rootedness and their provision of shelter and timber. Today's word "beam" was old English for both a living tree and a wooden post, or plank. This etymological origin is still revealed in the tree names hornbeam (*Carpinus betulus*), quickbeam (*Sorbus aucuparia*), and whitebeam (*Sorbus aria*). The German and Dutch words for tree, *Baum* and *boom*, are closely related to the old English *bēam*, and etymologists have further suggested their connection to the Indo-Germanic terms for growing and building.[28]

On the scale of entire cities, since the second half of the 19th century, municipal governments have initiated the systematic inclusion of plants in parks and the planting of street trees, realizing the various health benefits trees offer through their climatic and aesthetic functions. Providing a green infrastructure, these tree networks are interwoven with the urban fabric. Trees have naturalized cities, while they themselves—through adaptation to the urban straight jacket and conditions—have been urbanized. In many instances, urban trees have survived the destruction of entire cities, outlived crises and catastrophes, and they have come to symbolize resilience, survival, and rebirth. For example, a Callery pear, the "survivor tree" that endured the September 11 attacks on New York City's World Trade Center in 2001, has become a revered memorial at the site of terror, loss, and destruction. Hiroshima's legendary hibaku trees survived the atomic bomb blast of August 6, 1945. In Berlin after the Second World War, numerous old trees belonged to the city's oldest heritage, prompting one journalist to note that a botanical perspective was necessary to find traces of the old Berlin.[29]

Protection

Human life is impossible without plant life. If we are to survive, now more than ever before, plants will need our care, protection, and management, despite their resilience. It is, for example, unclear for how long we will still be able to stand awe-struck in front of a more than 3,000-year-old giant sequoia in California, rather than only marvel at it in Mielck's and other representations. The Italian futurists' early-20th-century utopian, or perhaps rather dystopian, vision for a world of artificial vegetation and smells, and the plastic shrubs and palms actually "planted" over half a century later in 1972, along more than 1.5 miles of Los Angeles's Jefferson Boulevard, were untenable simulacra.[30] Fedele Azari's 1924 manifesto for a "futurist flora" in abstract shapes and strong colors and smells suggested a virile proactive takeover of what was construed as an outdated natural flora with female traits like delicate colors. "Planting" naturalistic plastic shrubs and palms along Los Angeles roadways was a desperate reaction revealing both governmental incompetence and an environmental crisis it was insufficiently addressing. The artificial vegetation appeared, as one journalist argued, as "a sort of Madame Tussaud's of nature" that recalled "what once was, before progress triumphed."[31]

Although plants lie at the center of landscape architecture's conservative impulse, it is possible for landscape architecture to overcome it by contributing both to protecting plants and nonhuman nature more generally, and to creating comfortable and healthy future living spaces for humanity at large. In the early 19th century, British landscape gardener Loudon offered two visionary examples. Both designs were circular and open-ended, accommodating transformation and perpetual growth. They were kinetic not static, and they could be extended indefinitely. In his 1812 prototypical design for a botanical garden, the center was marked by a monumental glass house. Spiraling outwards was a pathway accompanied by amorphous beds for plants arranged according to Linnaeus's system. Spaces were left between the planting beds so that species discovered in the future could be integrated without changing the general design.[32] It is this flexibility and the ability to adapt that we do not only find in plants themselves but that has become increasingly important in landscape design, especially in times of climate change. In Loudon's 1829 conceptual design for London's expansion entitled "Hints for Breathing Places," circular greenbelts including parks, gardens, and forests alternated with urban fabric.[33] Loudon suggested that his concept could also be applied to "a capital for an Australian Union."[34] George Strickland Kingston and William Light's 1837 city plan for Adelaide included greenbelts that, however, were as much health precaution as the colonists' barrier and separation from indigenous lands, thus providing another example of landscape's duplicity.

In contrast to many of his contemporaries Loudon was not against growth and urbanization, but he wanted it to occur in an orderly and healthy way, securing access to vegetated areas for the entire population. Half a century after the discovery of photosynthesis—at the time also described as the capacity of plants "to correct bad air, and to improve good air"[35]—it was clear that the increasingly congested and industrialized cities needed plants to filter, clean, and provide "fresh" air for its human inhabitants. Dutch biologist John Ingenhousz, whose experiments had shed light on plants' gas exchange in the late 18th century, had pointed out that it was also relevant which kinds of trees should be planted for this purpose.[36]

Whereas evolutionary processes and plant breeding (since the 20th century this has included mutation breeding and genetic engineering) have produced new cultivars on the scale of the individual plant, on the planetary scale plants have become building materials for geoengineering. Greenbelts envisioned by Loudon on a metropolitan and regional scale in the early 19th century became shelterbelts and antidesertification measures spanning entire nations, even continents, in the 20th century. The United States' Great Plains Shelterbelt in the 1930s was to protect against dust storms and droughts. Similarly, the USSR's Great Plan for the Transformation of Nature included a network of shelterbelts across its southern steppes in the 1940s, and China's Three-North Shelter Forest Program was begun in the 1970s to prevent the expansion of the Gobi Desert. Today's transcontinental African Great Green Wall project in the Sahel zone that seeks to improve food security and includes tree planting began with a continent-spanning tree planting idea in the 1950s. Despite their varying degrees of success, these geoengineering projects have accentuated plants' radical agency and potential on a global scale. As philosopher Emanuele Coccia has reminded us, given plants' role in creating an atmosphere that enables animal life on the planet in the first place, plants "change the world, not just their environment or their ecological niche."[37]

Today's large-scale tree planting campaigns, whether in or outside cities, are motivated in large part by concerns about the planet at large and its changing climate. While atmospheric CO_2 has been measured since the early 19th century and the influence of the human-induced rise of CO_2 levels on climate has been theorized since the late 19th century, only since the 1950s have regular measurements affirmed the theory and raised concerns. A sea change occurred. Until the 1930s, scientists exploring connections between CO_2 levels and climate considered temperature rise a positive development – after all, it could make temperatures in the Northern Hemisphere more amenable for human life and raise crop production "for the benefit of rapidly propagating humankind."[38] This belief was increasingly questioned after the

Second World War once humans' harmful impact on their environment became undeniable and many feared that atmospheric nuclear testing was changing the weather.[39] Although the theory posed that plants' ability to sequester carbon was significant only temporarily because sequestered carbon returned to the atmosphere from the biosphere within a time frame of 10 to 250 years,[40] plants were considered immediately as potential palliatives and carbon sinks against global warming. The president of the American Association for the Advancement of Science Chauncey D. Leake suggested in a paper given at the 1958 National Conference on Air Pollution in Washington, DC, that perhaps "10 trees planted for every automobile, with 100 for every truck, would help," and he surmised that cities could "certainly benefit from such tree planting."[41] His proposal came only some months after meteorologist Charles David Keeling had begun to measure atmospheric carbon dioxide at Hawaii's Mauna Loa Observatory in spring 1958, ultimately confirming that CO_2 levels were rising steadily and were associated with emissions from the burning of fossil fuels.[42] It took until the 1970s for physicist Freeman J. Dyson to elaborate on Leake's idea in his 1976 proposal to use large-scale tree planting and the intensive cultivation of water hyacinths for artificial peat production as "emergency plant-growing programs" to produce "carbon banks." Far from being a solution to the

threat of global warming, Dyson, who in the last decades of his life turned to question its harmful effects, saw in plants "a stop-gap measure to hold the atmospheric CO_2 level down for a few decades and buy time in which a permanent shift from reliance on fossil fuels to renewable photosynthetic (or nuclear) fuels can be completed."[43]

However, plants' value lies not only in their CO_2 sequestration, urban heat island mitigation, and stormwater management, but also in the habitats they offer, the meanings they carry, the various senses they enliven and inspire, and the empathy they induce among humans toward nonhuman nature and the environment more generally. As Pliny the Elder wrote in the first century CE, "[Nature] had given already the soft plants...that make pleasant foods; she had coloured the remedies in flowers, and by the mere sight had attracted our attention, combining the helpful with what is actually delightful."[44] If, as Coccia has argued, plants turned the earth into "the metaphysical space of breath,"[45] landscape architects are among the shapers, cultivators, and keepers of that breath.

1. H. Rackham, Pliny *Natural History with an English Translation in Ten Volumes, Volume 5* (libri XVII–XIX), book 17, chapter 15: 77, chapter 36: 199–203, 210–14.

2. For an early description of the mural, see A. Mau, "Scavi di Pompei 1894–95," *Mittheilungen des Kaiserlich Deutschen Archäologischen Instituts, Römische Abtheilung* 11 (Loescher & Co., 1896), 1–97 (81–82).

3. *Caelibus*, the Latin word to describe single, widowed, and divorced men, was also used to describe trees that did not support vines. See, e.g., Rackham, Pliny, book 17, chapter 35: 204.

4. Heinrich von Salisch, *Forstästhetik* (Julius Springer, 1885).

5. Anne Whiston Spirn, *The Language of Landscape* (New Haven and London: Yale University Press, 1998).

6. Sonja Dümpelmann, *Seeing Trees: A History of Street Trees in New York City and Berlin* (Yale University Press, 2019), 41.

7. Sonja Dümpelmann, "'La battaglia del fiore.' Gardens, Parks and the City in Fascist Italy," *Studies in the History of Gardens and Designed Landscapes* 25, no. 1 (2005): 40–70.

8. See Gert Gröning Joachim & Wolschke-Bulmahn, "The Myth of Plant-Invaded Gardens and Landscapes," *Etudes Rurales* 185 (2010): 197–218.

9. John Claudius Loudon, *An Encyclopaedia of Gardening* (London: Longman et al., 1822), 1076.

10. Ibid., 1077; Sonja Dümpelmann, "Plant(s) Matter: On the Dichotomy and Duplicity of Green Walls and Pavements," in Franca Trubiano et al. (eds), *Bio Matter Technics Synthetics* (Actar, 2022).

11. Stephen Daniels, "Marxism, culture, and the duplicity of landscape," in Richard Peet & Nigel Thrift (eds), *New Models in Geography: The Political-Economy Perspective* (Unwin Hyman, 1989), 196–220 (196, 206).

12. Daniels, "Marxism," 206.

13. *The Natural History of Pliny*, trans. John Bostock & H.T. Riley (Henry G. Bohn, 1856), vol. IV, book 19, chapter 1, 129; book 20, chapter 1, 206.

14. James H. Wandersee & Elisabeth

E. Schussler, "Toward a Theory of Plant Blindness," *Plant Science Bulletin* 47, no. 1 (2001): 2–9.

15. Francis Hallé, *In Praise of Plants* (Timber Press, 2002 [1999]), 23–40.

16. On the connection between racial and gender discrimination, and the disregard of plants and horticulture in landscape architectural education, see Sonja Dümpelmann, "Landscape Gardening, Landscape Architecture, and Outdoor Art: The Beginning of Landscape Architectural Education in the United States 1862–1920" in Stefanie Hennecke & Diedrich Bruns (eds), *Landscape Architecture Education History. Educators–Schools–Methods–Curricula* (Routledge, forthcoming).

17. Marder, *Plant Thinking: A Philosophy of Vegetal Life* (Columbia University Press, 2013), 3–4.

18. Matthew Hall, *Plants as Persons: A Philosophical Botany* (New York: State University of New York Press, 2011), 169.

19. Marder, *Plant Thinking*, 3, 9.

20. Dümpelmann, "Plant(s) Matter."

21. W. Marshall Darley, "The Essence of 'Plantness,'" *The American Biology Teacher* 52, no. 6 (1990): 354–57.

22. Luce Irigaray, "What the Vegetal World Says to Us," in Monica Gagliano et al. (eds), *The Language of Plants: Science, Philosophy, Literature* (University of Minnesota Press, 2019), 126–35 (133–34).

23. Frederick Law Olmsted, *Walks and Talks of an American Farmer in England* (Putnam & Co., 1852), 133.

24. Frederick Law Olmsted, "The Spoils of the Park," cit. in Frederick Law Olmsted Jr. & Theodora Kimball (eds), *Frederick Law Olmsted Landscape Architect 1922–1903: Central Park* (New York and London: Putnam's Sons, 1928), 117–55 (144).

25. See, e.g., Marc-Rajan Köppler et al., "Enhancing wasteland vegetation by adding ornamentals: Opportunities and constraints for establishing steppe and prairie species on urban demolition sites," *Landscape and Urban Planning* 126 (2014): 1–9.

26. Eduard Mielck, *Die Riesen der Pflanzenwelt* (Winter'sche Verlagsbuchhandlung, 1863), figure XVI, 121–23.

27. Mielck, *Pflanzenwelt*, 124.

28. "beam" in the *Oxford English Dictionary*, "Baum," and "bauen," in Friedrich Kluge (ed.), *Etymologisches Wörterbuch der deutschen Sprache* (De Gruyter, 2012), 97–98.

29. Sonja Dümpelmann, "Trees, Wood, and Paper: Materialities of Urban Arboriculture in Modern Berlin," *Journal of Urban History* 46, no. 2 (2020): 310–33.

30. See, e.g., "Take That, Joyce Kilmer," Los Angeles Times (February 8, 1972), C6; Mike Goodman, "Valley Garden Groups Rap Plastic Plantings: Drive Launched to Squash," *Los Angeles Times* (February 8, 1972), SF6.

31. "Take That, Joyce Kilmer."

32. John Claudius Loudon, *Hints on the Formation of Gardens and Pleasure Grounds* (Printed for Gale, Curtis, and Fenner, 1813), 30.

33. John Claudius Loudon, "Hints for Breathing Places for the Metropolis, and for Country Towns and Villages, on fixed Principles," *The Gardener's Magazine* 5 (1829): 686–90.

34. Ibid., 688.

35. John Ingenhousz, *Experiments upon Vegetables* (London, 1779), 12.

36. Ibid., 93.

37. Emanuele Coccia, *The Life of Plants: A Metaphysics of Mixture* (Polity, 2019), 39.

38. Svante Arrhenius (1906), cit. in James Rodger Fleming, *Historical Perspectives on Climate Change* (Oxford University Press, 1998), 74.

39. Fleming, Climate Change, 118.

40. See Gilbert N. Plass, "The Carbon Dioxide Theory of Climatic Change," *Tellus* 8, no. 2 (1956): 140–54. Plass had presented his theory at the 122nd National Meeting of the American Meteorological Society in 1953; see, *Bulletin of the American Meteorological Society* 34, no. 2 (1953): 78–87.

41. Chauncey D. Leake, cit. in Dümpelmann, *Seeing Trees*, 242.

42. On the Keeling Curve, see Joshua P. Howe, *Behind the Curve: Science and the Politics of Global Warming* (University of Washington Press, 2014).

43. Freeman J. Dyson, "Can We Control the Carbon Dioxide in the Atmosphere?" *Energy* 2 (1977): 287–91 (291).

44. Rackham, *Pliny*, book 22, chapter 7: 16.

45. Coccia, *Plants*, 36.

ANIMALS

Richard Weller

Richard J. Weller is professor and chair of landscape architecture and co-executive director of the Ian L. McHarg Center for Urbanism and Ecology at the University of Pennsylvania where he also holds the Meyerson Chair of Urbanism. He is author or editor of eight books and his design work has been exhibited in major galleries including the Guggenheim in New York, the MAXXI Gallery in Rome, the Isabella Stewart Gardner Museum in Boston, and the Museum of Contemporary Art in Sydney. Weller's recent research on global flashpoints between urbanism and biodiversity has been widely published, while the related design work was exhibited at the 2021 Venice Biennale of Architecture.

Probably to survive being attacked, 600 million years ago some eukaryotic cells found it advantageous to band together and form larger assemblages. Epithelial cells then folded themselves into gastrula, essentially tubes with what we now refer to as a mouth at one end and an ass at the other. Around this fundamental morphology, evolution has sculpted an almost infinite array of fleshy forms. Of all these minor miracles we are but one, and although we know we are, as Darwin put it, "all netted together," we still like to tell ourselves we are the exceptional ones.[1] Unlike other animals we have words, numbers, foresight, free will, society, cities, and above all, gods.

Extraordinarily, we are also the first species in history to name an entire geological era after itself. But if we take the Anthropocene as an indictment rather than triumph, as I think we should, then our exceptionalism must now come under interrogation. As the Australian ethnographer Deborah Bird Rose renders it:

> The legacies of Western machinism have manifested through repeated assertions of human exceptionalism – that man is the only animal to make tools, that man is the only animal with language, a sense of fairness, generosity, laughter, that man is the only mindful creature. On the one hand all of these claims to exceptionalism have all been thoroughly undermined. On the other hand the term Anthropocene reminds us that it is not yet time to jettison a sense of human exceptionalism. Instead, by foregrounding the exceptional damage that humans are causing, the Anthropocene shows us the need for radically reworked forms of attention to what marks the human species as different.[2]

A cornerstone of constructing human identity throughout history has been our alleged differences from animals. It is little wonder then that so much recent scholarship has returned to the question of the animal with renewed scrutiny of what it means to be human. Indeed, on the occasion of their extinction, animals are suddenly everywhere.

The ascendance of Human-Animal Studies (HAS) in the humanities and with it the deconstruction of human exceptionalism, coincides generally with the growth of environmentalism over the course of the latter half of the 20th century. The origin of HAS can be pinpointed to the 1975 publication of

Peter Singer's *Animal Liberation: A New Ethics for our Treatment of Animals.*[3] Three years later, zoologists William McGrew and Caroline Tutin concluded in the journal *Man* that chimpanzees are not just smart animals but, like humans, actively construct a culture.[4] McGrew and Tutin's conclusion has since been controversially reinforced by others such as primatologist Sue Savage-Rumbaugh who claims that her research associate and coauthor, the bonobo "Kanzi," spontaneously learnt words in much the same way a child does.[5] It was also around this time that the stories of women such as Biruté Galdikas living with orangutans in Kalimantan, Jane Goodall living with chimpanzees in Tanzania, and Diane Fossey living (and dying) with gorillas in Rwanda entered popular culture.

Two years after McGrew and Tutin's scientific publication, philosophers Gilles Deleuze and Félix Guattari formulated their notion of "Becoming Animal" – inspiration perhaps for Jacques Derrida who left, on his death bed in 2004, an incomplete retort to Rene Descartes titled "The Animal That Therefore I Am." In anthropology two important recent books—*Beyond Nature and Culture*[6] by Philippe Descola and *How Forests Think: Towards an Anthropology of the Nonhuman*[7] by Eduardo Kohn—both published in 2013, build upon the legacy of Claude Lévis-Strauss's renowned investigations into animism. For Descola and Kohn animism is a way of circumventing, if not entirely reconciling, the problem of dualism in western thought. Whereas capitalism and its mechanistic underpinnings render the slaughter of millions of animals in so-called "concentrated animal feeding operations" invisible, animism sanctifies the highly selective and ritualistic killing of wild animals in relatively small numbers.

These scientific, philosophical, and anthropological reorientations have been consolidated in books such as Jennifer Wolch and Jody Emel's 1998 *Animal Geographies*[8] followed by Julie Urbanik's 2012 *Placing Animals.*[9] Two years later, the *Routledge Handbook of Animal Studies*[10] was published and most recently, in 2018, Lori Gruen—a professor of ethics at Wesleyan College—published *Critical Terms for Animal Studies.*[11] Under the rubric of environmental humanities, HAS is also now being keyed into the general discourse of the Anthropocene where, for example, in books such as *Art in the Anthropocene* by Etienne Turpin and Heather Davies[12] and *Arts of Living on a Damaged Planet*[13] by Anna Tsing, artists, scientists, and sociologists, among others, are coming together to define the zeitgeist as decidedly more-than-human.

At the same time that animals have risen to prominence in ethics, philosophy, and anthropology, they have also been actively reimagined and strategically repositioned in visual arts and literature. In art, after centuries of almost total absence as subjects in their own right, a breakthrough occurred when, in 1969, Jannis Kounellis herded a dozen horses into the Galleris L'Attico in Rome. This was followed in 1974 by Joseph Beuys's performance at the Rene Block Gallery in New York where he spent a week inside a room with a coyote. In the same year William Wegman produced a film of himself giving his dog "Man Ray" a spelling lesson, a form of performance art he has continued to this day. And who could forget Damien Hirst's 14-foot tiger shark suspended in formaldehyde first displayed in 1991. Not without criticism, Hirst has since expanded his taxidermic menagerie to include no less than 27 more sharks, as well as large numbers of fish, sheep, cows, calves, bulls, horses, pigs, a brown bear, and his *coup de grace,* a whole zebra. Other artists such as the partnership of Olly Williams and Suzi Winstanley on the other hand, apply a different code of conduct to their engagement with animals; first, their animals are always alive, and second, they only make art about their subjects while embedded in *their* habitat observing them as they go about their business.[14] Unlike Hirst who farms his work out to fisherman, Olly and Suzi literally swim with sharks while trying to draw them.

This emphasis on processes of life rather than products of death is developed further by Natalie Jeremijenko who gathers her artwork under the title "OOZ." Jeremijenko works to the rule that any action you can direct at an animal, the animal can direct back at you. Instead of packaging art for galleries, Jeremijenko constructs elaborate theatrical, quasi-experimental events to bring animals, plants, and people together and emphasize the urban ecological networks they are all a part of. For example, her 2012 project *Salamander Superhighway* is a small pipe set within a speed bump across a road near the Socrates

Sculpture Park in New York that provides safe passage for migrating salamanders. As they move through the superhighway they trigger a sensor that sends tweets to humans such as, "Hi Honey, I'm heading home."[15]

In literature, perhaps best known is Elizabeth Kolbert's 2014 book *The Sixth Extinction*, which outlined the loss of biodiversity in a way that caught the public's attention and became a bestseller.[16] In two more recent books—*Being a Beast*[17] by the philosopher and veterinarian Charles Foster and *Goat Man*[18] by Thomas Thwaites—the authors regale their respective attempts to not only live *with* but also live *like* their animal subjects. Eating worms and digging burrows, Foster temporarily "became" a badger. He has also lived as an otter, an urban fox, a red deer, and a swift. For his field work Thwaites disguised himself as a goat replete with custom-made prosthetics to walk on all fours so as to be accepted into a wild goat community.

So, what about the status of the animal in design culture? Apart from the established genre of designing zoological enclosures that can only reiterate or disguise the domination of the human gaze, that animals would even be considered a subject of design outside of zoos has been, until recently, uncommon. Consequently, MVRDV's provocative "Pig City," a high-rise pig farm designed in 2001 came as something of a shock.[19] But here the issue was not so much one of animal rights or a concern with human identity in relation to animals, rather it was one of pragmatically reducing the sprawling footprint of Dutch pork production. From the animal's perspective it likely matters naught whether the concrete floor plate of the slaughterhouse is single or stacked. As Temple Grandin, an animal behaviorist with an uncanny ability to empathize with ruminants, highlighted, what matters is the animal's experience in that slaughterhouse. She designed a new, more "humane" way of guiding cattle through the horrors of the modern abattoir to their endpoint.

We prefer of course to look at picturesque landscapes with wild animals, especially from the comforts of our living rooms or from designer hideaways.

One of the most photogenic of these in recent times is surely the Norwegian Wild Reindeer Centre Pavilion located at Hjerkinn on the outskirts of Dovrefjell National Park. Designed by Snøhetta, the pavilion is a masterclass in the architectural craft of ecotourism, but it does little to challenge conventional human-nonhuman relations. Neither do the barges tethered to Pier 39 in San Francisco on which hundreds of wild sea lions sunbathe. And yet, the integration of the sea lion herd into the general hubbub of an active port is a happy and unusual instance of the ideal that cities could be places of cohabitation. Lolling about in the sun, oblivious to the crowds who gather to marvel at their otherness, the sea lions seem to satisfy Jennifer Wolch's call "to renaturalize cities and invite the animals back in and in the process re-enchant the city."[20] For Wolch this re-enchantment is not just for human pleasure, it is "to allow for the emergence of an ethic, practice, and politics of caring for animals and nature."[21]

While many landscape projects may well be unintentionally good for a range of species, outside of zoos there are few that have been explicitly designed *for* – let alone *with* animals. Exceptions include a 1990s West 8 icon, the Eastern Scheldt storm surge barrier in Holland made from large swathes of black and white shells,[22] intended to be conducive to the nesting habits of local birds. More recently, Ken Smith has made a fun dog park on the East River waterfront of New York;[23] JCFO has detailed the edge of the Seattle waterfront so as to create a safe haven for salmon;[24] Kate Orff has put oysters to work off the coast of Staten Island, New York, to buffer storm surge;[25] and MVVA may yet build the ARC Wildlife Overpass in Vail, Colorado.[26]

The lack of design *for* animals in landscape architecture is matched by a dearth of writing on the topic.[27] Seeking to address this deficiency, Kevan Klosterwill, writing in *Landscape Journal*, set out the topic in three parts: the scenic animal, the systematic animal, and the social animal.[28] In broad brush strokes he mapped each of these onto the history of landscape architecture from the 18th century to today. The scenic animal relates to the ways in which primarily agricultural animals were discussed by connoisseurs in relation to the aesthetics of the aristocratic English landscape. But so too we could include in this category the 19th- and 20th-century creation of national parks and the faux naturalism of 20th- and early-21st-century zoological enclosures. The systematic animal is that which is subsumed into landscape planning based on landscape ecology. This is the landscape of corridors, patches, conservation easements, and protected areas planned according to multi-species networks and wildlife population dynamics. Finally, the social animal relates to design that seeks "cohabitation and collaboration where humans play a less than dominant role" and to unsettle "the logic of nature and culture on which many conservation ideas were privileged."[29] In other words, designing for the social animal means bringing contemporary landscape architecture and HAS together in challenging the exceptionalism of the human subject. And since the act of design is typically considered a quintessential feature of that exceptionalism, it means that the way in which we design must itself be questioned.

This was the premise of the LA+ CREATURE design competition held by the Weitzman School of Design's flagship journal *LA+* in 2020. The 258 entries received provide insights into how designers around the world are currently thinking about the status of the animal in their work.[30] Instead of trying to squeeze these entries into Klosterwill's categories (scenic, systemic, and social), I propose an aesthetically more suggestive taxonomy of Rewilds,

Green Machines, and Monsters. Projects falling into the Rewilds category typically situated the animal as a victim of human ignorance and exploitation and sought to correct this through the application of the principles of landscape ecology to sizable tracts of land and water. These projects tried to win back land from agriculture, urbanization, and infrastructure in order to make room for the animal and its habitat. Aesthetically, the Rewilds were typically presented in an arcadian, pastoral, and picturesque manner, foregrounding a rebounding, naturalistic ecosystem where any evidence of the technology involved in its recreation is rendered invisible. In these images the animal is the hero, but the human also plays a role; no longer wreaking havoc, now a caring steward helping the land and threatened species through a process of healing. In short, this is the world envisaged by the conservation movement, and while it is crucially important at the landscape scale in urban contexts it can lapse into a reification of nature that reinforces rather than reimagines the dualism of culture and nature that is in fact causal to the environmental crisis in the first place.

 Instead of decoupling culture and nature as the Rewilds would have it, the Green Machines accepted and tried to work with the contemporary city and all its related infrastructure as the basis of a new nature. In this schema the city is reconceptualized as a novel ecosystem, one that could—if it were innovatively designed and retrofitted—serve both humans and nonhumans and bring the two closer together. The Green Machines can also be designs applied to specific environmental problems well beyond the actual city. For example, if, because of human-induced changes, walruses can no longer navigate through the arctic we just design a machine—say a remote-controlled barge covered in manufactured ice—to help them do so. Aesthetically, the Green Machines are less concerned with restoring a certain landscape in the image of natural nature as they are with utilizing and foregrounding technology's capacity to solve ecological problems and help streamline ecosystem services. This is the world of greener and smarter cities where the myth that design can solve most, if not all, of our problems is alive and well.

The projects that I refer to as the Monsters are perhaps the most interesting; they are less romantic than the Rewilds and more suspicious of a designed future than the Green Machines. Emerging from a critical, post-human, post-natural sensibility that now permeates the humanities and the art world, these are projects that actively seek to destabilize anthropocentrism and incite indeterminate, amoral processes of evolutionary change. The aesthetic of this approach is typically inclined toward the cyborgian, the dystopian, and the grotesque. Often from within the political milieu of ecofeminism and eco-socialism their creators are critical of modernity and its manifestation in the climate crisis of the scientific and corporate state and equate the exploitation of animals with the exploitation of people. Design can't necessarily fix the world's ecological problems—indeed to even read the situation as a problem requiring a fix is to be part of the problem—but it can open our minds and bodies to transformative experiences that are in themselves considered a form of prerequisite for socio-political change and an acceleration of evolution's creativity.

Each of these categories—the Rewilds, the Green Machines, and the Monsters—has its own preferred scale: respectively large, medium, and small. Each category also has its own mythos: respectively the paradisiacal, the ecotopian, and the dystopian. The challenge for landscape architecture as a spatial practice in relation to the animal is, I think, to work across the grain of all three at once. If we are to have any hope of broaching the sixth extinction, then design must—to return to Klosterwill—interconnect the scenic, the systemic, and the social. At Penn over the last eight years I have been concerned with how to do this in terms of curating my own research so that it might make a meaningful contribution to the global conservation community's efforts to protect and enhance biodiversity. Since the mid-20th century, conservation efforts have generally resulted in the creation of protected areas. With the oversight of the International Union for the Conservation of Nature (IUCN) these lands now amount to just over one-fifth of the world's terrestrial area – and although this "land grab" is not without its critics and contradictions, it is by any measure an extraordinary achievement.

The problem from a long-term ecological perspective, however, is that the global estate of protected areas is an archipelago of isolated and ad hoc fragments. This makes it almost impossible to achieve the intent of the two key words in the Convention on Biological Diversity: representation and connectivity. Representation means that instead of setting aside, say, a vast area of land in Siberia, protected areas should represent the world's biological diversity more or less equally across its 867 ecoregions. Connectivity means that, ideally, protected areas would be connected into larger landscape networks so that species can migrate over time to adjust to the pressures of climate change. Achieving connectivity means building landscape corridors of restored habitat through areas of land use typically hostile to biodiversity. If the 196 nations that are parties to the Convention on Biological Diversity are serious about meeting their protected area targets and achieving representation and connectivity, they should come together to effectively reorganize land use on a global scale.

This, of course, is highly unlikely, but perhaps design thinking as opposed to only scientific and political approaches might be able to help. The design problem is to decide where and how greater connectivity and greater representation in the global conservation estate can be achieved. In seeking to provide a solution to this design problem, my research has focused on projects at two scales: first, at a planetary scale is the World Park Project; and second, at a regional scale, is the Hotspot Cities Project. Instead of just adding more fragments of protected area in an ad hoc manner, The World Park Project[31] galvanizes and concentrates the global conservation effort to create over 160,000 square kilometers of contiguous, restored habitat through many of the world's biodiversity hotspots. The World Park begins with three trails, the first from Patagonia to Alaska, the second from Australia to Morocco, and the third from Namibia to Turkey. These trails are located to link the maximum number of protected areas in the maximum number of biodiversity hotspots. The trails are low-investment catalysts intended to attract people into these regions, not only as tourists but also as workers engaged in the World Park's bigger mission of restoring degraded landscapes in between existing protected areas so as to create connectivity. Whereas old-school conservation typically saw humans as threats to be excluded, the World Park—in this, the decade of ecological restoration—actively engages people in its creation and management.

At a finer scale, the Hotspot Cities Project[32] addresses the problem that over 90% of major cities (defined as 300,000 people or more) in the world's biodiversity hotspots are sprawling in direct conflict with endangered species. The premise of this work is that urban sprawl and the degradation of peri-urban landscapes is not a *fait accompli*; it can be mitigated by urban planning and urban design that includes a genuine concern for biodiversity. Biodiversity doesn't just mean charismatic animals and attractive flora, it encompasses entire ecosystems; for without healthy ecosystems, there can be no healthy cities, and without healthy cities there can be no healthy society. Barricading isolated pockets of land against urban growth—so-called "fortress conservation"—is ultimately ecologically untenable. It is also philosophically flawed because it recapitulates a worldview where culture is one thing, and nature another. This dualism is not how the world works, and nor is it actually the world we live in. We need, then, to also come at the problem of habitat loss from the urban side of the equation and redesign urban growth so that cities can become symbiotic with their landscapes rather than parasitic. In the Hotspot Cities Project we have not only identified which cities are sprawling destructively into their neighboring lands, we have also conducted case studies showing how urban design can integrate biodiversity with the needs of urban growth.[33] When we put the World Park and Hotspot Cities projects together it is possible to see how, from the scale of urban neighborhoods to the scale of the planet, it is possible to create an integrated network of landscapes that supports more-than-human life.

1. The full quote reads, "If we choose to let conjecture run wild, then animals, our fellow brethren in pain, diseases, death, suffering, and famine—our slaves in the most laborious works, our companions in our amusements—they may partake [of] our origin in one common ancestor – we may be all netted together": Charles Darwin, *The Descent of Man and Selection in Relation to Sex* (Penguin Classics, 2004; first published by John Murray, 1871), 126.

2. Deborah Bird Rose, "Shimmer: When all you Love is Being Trashed" in Anna Tsing, et al. (eds), *Arts of Living on a Damaged Planet: Ghosts and Monsters* (University of Minnesota Press, 2017), 52.

3. Peter Singer, *Animal Liberation: A New Ethics for our Treatment of Animals* (Harper Perennial, 1975).

4. William C. McGrew & Caroline Tutin, "Evidence for a Social Custom in Wild Chimpanzees?" *Man* 13, no. 2 (1973): 234–52.

5. Sue Savage-Rumbaugh, et al., "Welfare of Apes in Captive Environments: Comments On, and By, a Specific Group of Apes," *Journal of Applied Animal Welfare Science* 10, no. 1 (2007): 7–19.

6. Philippe Descola, *Beyond Nature and Culture* (University of Chicago Press, 2013).

7. Eduardo Kohn, *How Forests Think: Toward an Anthropology of the Nonhuman* (University of California Press, 2013).

8. Jennifer R. Wolch & Jody Emel (eds), *Animal Geographies: Place, Politics, and Identity in the Nature-Culture Borderlands* (Verso, 1998).

9. Julie Urbanik, *Placing Animals: An Introduction to the Geography of Human-Animal Relations* (Rowman and Littlefield Publishers, 2012).

10. Garry Marvin & Susan McHugh, *Handbook of Animal Studies* (Routledge, 2014).

11. Lori Gruen, *Critical Terms for Animal Studies* (University of Chicago Press, 2018).

12. Etienne Turpin & Heather Davies, *Art in the Anthropocene: Encounters Among Aesthetics, Politics, Environments and Epistemologies* (Open Humanities Press, 2014).

13. Anna Tsing, et al. (eds), *Arts of Living on a Damaged Planet: Ghosts and Monsters* (University of Minnesota Press, 2017), 1–14.

14. OllySuzi, https://www.ollysuzi.com.

15. Suzanne Jacobs, "This artist is using technology to bring nature back into the city," *Grist* (November 9, 2015).

16. Elizabeth Kolbert, *The Sixth Extinction: An Unnatural History* (Henry Holt and Company, 2014).

17. Charles Foster, *Being a Beast: An Intimate and Radical Look at Nature* (Picador, 2016).

18. Thomas Thwaites, *Goat Man: How I Took a Holiday from being Human* (Princeton Architectural Press, 2016).

19. MVRDV, "Pig City," https://www.mvrdv.nl/projects/134/pig-city.

20. Jennifer R. Wolch, "Zoopolis" in Wolch & Emel (eds), *Animal Geographies*, 123.

21. Ibid., 124.

22. West 8, https://www.west8.com/projects/all/landscape_design_eastern_scheldt_storm_surge_barrier/.

23. Ken Smith Workshop, http://kensmithworkshop.com/erw-dog-run.html.

24. American Society of Landscape Architects, https://www.asla.org/2017awards/320768.html.

25. Scape, https://www.scapestudio.com/projects/oyster-tecture/.

26. ARC, https://arc-solutions.org.

27. There are two notable exceptions: Wolch & Emel (eds), *Animal Geographies*; and John Beardsley (ed.), *Designing Wildlife Habitats* (Harvard University Press, 2013).

28. Kevin Klosterwill, "The Shifting Position of Animals in Landscape Theory," *Landscape Journal* 38, no. 1–2 (2019): 129–46.

29. Ibid., 143.

30. See *LA+ Interdisciplinary Journal of Landscape Architecture*, CREATURE, no. 14 (2021). See also, https://laplusjournal.com/14-CREATURE.

31. The World Park, https://theworldpark.com.

32. The Hotspot Cities Project, https://hotspotcitiesproject.com.

33. Richard Weller, et al., "The Hotspot Cities Project: The Case Study of Bogotá 2050," *JoLA: Journal of Landscape Architecture* 16, no. 1 (2021) 76–89.

AGRICULTURE

Ellen Neises

Ellen Neises is the Laurie Olin Professor of Practice in Landscape Architecture and executive director of PennPraxis, the non-profit center for applied research and design practice at the University of Pennsylvania Weitzman School of Design. She works on large-scale and large-scope design problems involving land, water, and development at the intersection of physical and policy design. She organized the Farm of the Future symposium (2021) in collaboration with the Penn Veterinary School to advance research and diffusion of innovations for humane, climate-sustainable agriculture.

Fifty percent of the planet's ice-free, habitable land surface has been cleared for crops, pasture, and rangeland.[1] In all likelihood this figure will continue to increase for much of this century. If biodiversity, climate change, human sustainability, and stewardship are core concerns of landscape architecture, then the agricultural landscape must be part of its purview. This essay summarizes the problems of contemporary production agriculture and explores the question of whether food systems are amenable to design, identifying openings for design agency at a range of scales, and linking those openings to the history of the design of agricultural landscapes. The aim is to reflect critically on whether landscape architects engaged in evidence-based design can lay out pathways to policy reform and spatial change that construct alternative futures in this complex milieu. I will concentrate on the US, but many of the observations and strategies apply internationally.

Nothing since the last ice age has been more disruptive to ecosystems and biodiversity than agriculture. Expansion of land area under cultivation over the last 50 years has led to a steep decline in habitat acreage. Water use for agriculture has had a major impact on availability of drinking water and water resources for trees and plants that support biodiversity, carbon sequestration, cooling, air quality, and other ecosystem services. In the United States, for example, farming accounts for 80% of the country's consumptive use of water, and 90% of consumptive use in some western states.[2] Aquifer reserves are being depleted and surface waters diverted, creating tension between cities and agricultural counties, between states and nations, between cultivated and wild.

Major shifts in practice over the last 50 years compound the land and water use crises. These include shifts to monocultural planting without rotation; regional specialization in livestock or crops (not both) and subsequent atrophy of non-specialist supply chains; genetic selection and simplification of stock; maximization of short-term yields by large agribusinesses that rent land, contract with growers, and have no self-interest in maintaining soil fertility; government subsidy of water, transportation carbon, and commodity prices; and heavy reliance on industrial fertilizers, pesticides, selective herbicides, and animal medications to increase productivity and reduce labor. The increase in fertilizer use pushed environmental loads of nitrogen and phosphorus beyond biophysical thresholds for planetary health more than a decade ago, and scientists fear we are approaching catastrophic tipping points in the degradation of lakes, rivers, estuaries, and aquifers.[3]

Taken as a whole, the food system we have created—including production, processing, and distribution of food—is responsible for 26% of global greenhouse gas emissions.[4] Because agriculture occupies so much land, it also competes with climate actions that require territory, like expanding renewable energy or forestry. Without radical redesign, rising demand for farm products will push emissions up substantially. Population growth (currently +81 million people per year worldwide), increased demand for biofuel, and the decline of world fisheries are expected to double or even triple demand for agricultural production over the next 30 to 40 years, placing huge pressure on resources and emissions management, and increasing the risk of famine.

It would be one thing if this massive allocation of land, water, and carbon created a food system that was equitable, healthy, biosecure, respectful of animal welfare, delicious, and aesthetically inspiring, but it has not. In many countries, we have created two food systems: one elite and one affordable. The elite system produces well-made food and sustainable farms, and joyful preoccupation with a food scene that diverts our attention from the real food landscapes out there. Meanwhile, the vast, mass-market food system creates profoundly adverse impacts on the environment and almost all its human and animal participants.

The Problem with Agribusiness Food Systems

In many production agriculture and food systems, we have optimized cheap food at enormous cost to the health of humans, animals, and the earth. While farmers and farm policy get all the attention when environmental improvements are discussed, the structure of the food system, income inequality, and the absence of effective environmental regulation and industrial zoning code for production agriculture are rarely part of the public conversation. The impacts of production agriculture vary from place to place based on the crop or type of livestock, but the structure of the system has become increasingly uniform. Farmers now face highly concentrated, monopolistic markets for seeds, chemicals, food processing, slaughter, and retailing. National and international food chains force their growers—an expendable labor force working on short-term contracts and leased land—to accept low profit margins that require growers to hyper-specialize and mass-produce to survive.[5] Agribusinesses, in effect, assign specialist roles in production agriculture to whole regions, making sustainable closed loops geographically impossible.

In "Who 'Designs' the Agricultural Landscape?" conservation biologist Laura Jackson argues that agricultural landscapes have been continuously re-engineered and redesigned for short-term efficiency.[6] Jackson shows how sites of industrial agriculture are shaped by aggressive agribusiness strategy, weak policy and government incentives, and the uninformed preferences of most consumers. Jackson gives the example of the upper Midwest "Corn Belt" – the agricultural landscape that is most responsible for producing feed for animal protein in the US. This region is challenged by decaying communities and environmental collapse due to the intensive farming of corn and soybeans. A few signs of the impact on the local environment are that Iowa lakes and streams have measured among the highest nutrient levels in the world; the herbicide atrazine is so concentrated in surface waters that it is also found in the rain; and less than 0.1% of perennial tallgrass prairies remain to support insects and wildlife.[7] Corn Belt waterways displace much of the impact of chemically nurtured feed stock monocultures to the distant, downstream zone of hypoxia in the Gulf of Mexico. Midwest grain is consumed and converted to manure by animals in distant regions, in concentrations so high it is treated as waste rather than fertilizer because those agricultural regions are now specialists too.

The current design of Corn Belt agriculture—now optimized to create cheap feed and other industrial inputs—doesn't even make money for the region. Farmers' production costs regularly outstrip their receipts, and the region survives only because of federal subsidies and off-farm income. The region's population, social support systems, property values, commercial strips, and health are all in decline. Jackson notes that based on her personal observation, "Small town commerce is often paired down to just three businesses: the grain elevator/farm chemical store, the convenience store/gas station, and the bar."[8]

Prior to 1996, subsidy payments in the US were tied to conservation compliance and production limits, but environmental requirements have since been dropped or greatly relaxed. The few programs that reward farmers for multiple benefits to soil, wildlife, and water, like the Conservation Stewardship Program, are terribly unfunded – $2.2 billion in 2020 versus the $22 billion spent on subsidies without meaningful stewardship requirements. While the practices of most industries are guided by industrial zoning code and environmental regulation, the rules of production agriculture in the US are not effectively shaped by law or incentives.

The Corn Belt is not a wild outlier. A similar story can be told for many kinds of production agriculture in North America and other countries in advanced stages of consolidation. Careless animal agriculture generates the worst stories, but the impacts of vegetal agriculture on wildlife can be harsh as well. What is unique to the US is that we spend the least on food of any country in the world – only 6.4% of household income.[9] This means two things: first, we have succeeded in designing a food system that effectively optimizes an attribute (minimum cost); and second, you get what you pay for in a market economy. We can redesign and re-engineer the food system for a wider array of objectives – cost and quality, understood as environmental health plus animal welfare plus human health. This new, or old paradigm of the inseparability of human, animal, and earth health, which has become known as One Health, is not as elusive as it may seem.

An agribusiness executive with three decades of experience who spoke to me candidly in an interview in 2012 on the condition that I not quote him, had no trouble identifying which design parameters were flexible or predicting the agricultural future in Arizona and California 25 years hence. He said that as soon as government stopped subsidizing water, flood irrigation would cease, sprinkler irrigation would decline, and growers and their buyers would adopt and pay for low-flow drip irrigation except during germination. Not surprisingly to landscape architects, he said seed stock was highly mutable and seed could easily be disentangled from Round Up-ready formulations, GMO engineering, and adaptations for long-distance transportation to points of sale. Heirloom seed could be bulked and new sustainable varieties could be developed very rapidly. Disinvestment in the health of soil, water, insects, and animals, and toward chemicals, growth hormones, and antibiotics, would shift as soon as regulation or the market required it. If the government taxed labor less and machinery more, the means of production and wage levels would shift. If the primary source of research support for many land grant college agriculture programs was not agribusiness, researchers would return their attention to stewardship of the resources of each state. In big business, incentives and policy change behavior.

The Agency of Design in Food Systems

Agronomists, conservation biologists, and interdisciplinary teams that include landscape architects have used a variety of modeling techniques to determine that reintegrating crop and livestock systems on farms or in the farm region, and increasing crop diversity and the percentage of perennial cover measurably improve biodiversity, water quality, and the economy and quality of life in rural communities. Joan Nassauer and other landscape architects find, not surprisingly, that farmers prefer landscape scenarios that promote biodiversity and water resources.[10]

Through her Landscape Ecology, Perception, and Design Lab at the University of Michigan, Nassauer has developed a theory of the "cultural sustainability cycle" that gives design an important role in shaping perception of landscape and mobilizing action. "Landscape appearance, and particularly the appearance of care in landscapes, affects environmental health. To be successful and sustainable in the long run, ecological design requires both environmental and social science, *and* civic engagement."[11] Landscape pattern appearance matters, she says, because it links a culture to real functions of the environment. Landscape architects are important because we shape society's perception of the environment—what belongs and what needs to change—and that stimulates action. Design and communication can also shape people's perception of the feasibility of an approach at scale, where civic engagement supports the policies and preferences needed to create a new food system.

Even from this brief overview, we can see it isn't just the farmland that needs to be redesigned. The model of our food system needs to be reimagined, and the rural context and regional relationships of contemporary agriculture need design, planning, and policy attention. This won't happen through wishful visioning, but through rigor. All types of good cannot be maximized simultaneously as they often miraculously appear to be in landscape architectural representations. The challenge is to explore and quantify all the potentially acceptable tradeoffs between important values—maintaining concern for cost and economies of scale, and the risk carried by the people who cultivate our food—and to facilitate informed decision-making about the pricing (or prohibition) of inputs and impacts.[12]

We can help policymakers find this "solution space" through experiments in real physical places that become proven, charismatic examples by integrating aims, studying effects, and evaluating what tradeoffs between the multiple benefits we desire *mean*. Making and measuring alternative models of the production agriculture farm and food system in this way is what will allow us to achieve the cultural, political, and technical shift that will overwhelm the resistance of agribusiness to regulation in the public interest, support income access to humanely raised food, redirect government expenditures to incentivize sustainable farming, and align our appetites with survival.

Richard Buchanan writes in "Wicked Problems in Design Thinking" that designers—like systems thinkers—are generalists and integrators.[13] He says we are comfortable with indeterminacy and complexity. We are good at mining *the particular*, making exchanges between domains, and creating integrated solutions. Buchanan says designers have the right constitution for wicked systems problems, but not the patience or know-how to master the science and to shepherd projects through "the valley of death" of implementation and stewardship. He observes that government agencies financing applied research on most wicked problems have no idea what design can offer. A persistent problem is that "discussions between designers and members of the scientific community tend to leave little room for reflection on the broader nature of design…Instead of yielding productive integrations, the result is often confusion and breakdown of communication, with a lack of intelligent practice to carry innovative ideas into objective, concrete embodiment."[14] We need to build credibility and power as problem solvers, not just speculative futurists.

To influence relationships between food, water, habitat, animals, and people that could produce large-scale change, designers will have to get serious about the math and science, take a deep interest in the diffusion of innovation—getting to scale—and learn to integrate policy design and physical design of landscapes that unite function and expression. We will need to collaborate closely with agricultural planning, veterinary medicine, ecology, conservation biology, forestry, hydrology, systems analysis, carbon and soil science, regional planning, engineering, architecture, and social science. Our skill at drawing physical relationships connected with land and water at many scales will be useful in shifting culture and politics to make way for the new land practices, but we will need to recognize that the agency of design is different in the material sphere of agriculture than in the speculative and image-driven sphere of cities and real estate. Crops come in or they fail, bank notes are met or the farm is lost, and the biggest players will have one bottom line until, as the agribusiness executive said, the public interest is forcefully embedded in their practices and markets are made to reckon with their externalities.

From Theory to Practice

To make this real let's now turn to some projects that operate at a range of scales, and across a continuum from policy to site design. Taken together, these projects show some of the ways that we can more seriously engage the sites, economic structures, and points of leverage on mainstream agricultural production, to bring the largest land use on the planet within the purview of design, at scale.

Community-engaged think tank for national policy: The New Rural Economy Project (NREP), led by Concordia University and a dozen other schools, was an 11-year effort (1997 to 2008) to understand the rural economy and identify policy and strategy options at every scale from federal action to the single farm. The NREP was intended to inform the policymaking of Canada's federal Rural Secretariat, and to build rural capacity directly. The federal government selected 32 rural communities from across Canada to participate, and the Concordia team compared the economic capacity and challenges of each using diverse data sources and convening rural people, researchers, policy analysts, and businesses. Six of the eight key recommendations to localities that grew out of the NREP are things that designers know how to do: strengthen local identities, make interdependencies visible, identify and capitalize on the strategic advantages of the locality and region, increase environmental quality, welcome (and design for) newcomers, look to urban interests, and find ways to advance urban and rural interests jointly. The focus was not primarily on tourism (a weak economic driver in many contexts), but on quality of life and agricultural and economic diversification in an effort to reduce brain drain and attract in-migration. There was no design or physical planning element of the NREP, but had there been, the 32 communities might have gone further to realize these strategies. National policy in the form of intelligent incentives and appropriations could then have been informed by tested projects, increasing policy effectiveness and building consensus and stable investment.

Regional infrastructure: Highlands Hydroway is a proposal for multi-purpose, soft, distributed infrastructure in agricultural valleys in the New York metro-region to increase stormwater storage capacity, water quality, rate of aquifer recharge, quantity of biomass, and habitat value. The proposal[15] aims to demonstrate in one important geography that conservation of natural resources and rural economic development can be integrated in the design and management of high-performing, sustainable landscape infrastructure that stores and cleans huge quantities of water. Integration of engineering and ecology in infrastructure will create an example of multi-purpose, multi-municipal public works that elevate and connect agricultural communities.

Highland Hydroway seeks to advance a new economic model by initiating a catalytic, common project that creates resource exchange between the urban, suburban, and rural communities that share a watershed. Through that exchange, rural communities will earn the money they need to conserve the heritage of both working landscapes and important natural resource areas, and skilled rural people will "farm" ecosystem services for the region. As a result of their coordinated labor, and their quantifiable impact on flood flows and other ecosystem service outputs, urban communities will experience less flooding and dislocation; better drinking water, air quality, and cooling; and greater carbon sequestration and resource conservation. Through tools like transfer of development rights, conservation banks, and carbon markets, downstream cities can secure ecosystem services and flood storage upstream where they can be produced efficiently by rural people with the land, equipment, and know-how to manage soft infrastructure. Monetizing conservation work helps maintain the acreage of "greenfield" land in the New York metro area, a biodiverse region that is under enormous pressure from development.

Technical design: Jeremy Kaufman and the other young former farmers-turned-entrepreneurs who started Propagate Ventures have used systems thinking to support adoption of regenerative, diversified agriculture, one farm at a time.[16] For a consulting fee, they look at a farm property closely—its soils, slope, sun exposure, and other factors—and interview the farmers about what outputs they want to achieve, for example, increased profit on the same footprint, increased carbon sequestration to earn returns in carbon markets, more biodiversity, reduced erosion, or a combination of outputs. Then Propagate Ventures creates a physical layout of new crops and site modifications, a maintenance plan, and a spreadsheet that shows annual expenditures and returns over a 25-year period. Equipped with these tools, farmers can offer a business plan to potential investors or implement the diversification of their operations with loans or personal capital, with a clear understanding of risk, return, and especially, of cash flow.

If landscape architects were to give some form and expression to the silvopasture and orchards recommended by Propagate Ventures in order to increase their cultural power and legibility, this evidence-based design would be quite different from drawing aesthetically pleasing speculative propositions for farmers. The capacity to tailor technical recommendations to a site, quantify the output along a number of dimensions, and to specify and sequence inputs facilitates adoption of agroforestry and other sustainable techniques by (necessarily) risk-averse farmers. Together, technical design plus policy design will allow farmers to monetize innovation in payments for environmental impact units from revolving funds that enable action by many to reach scale.

Teaching and demonstration farms: Large animal veterinarians, landscape architects, hydrologists, agricultural conservation planners, and strategists are collaborating on the conversion of the Penn Veterinary School's 600-acre campus into The Farm of the Future – a demonstration campus that aims to stimulate widespread improvement in animal agriculture in the state of Pennsylvania and far beyond by promoting diffusion of innovation on many farms that shift practices to have more trees on the farm, more organic material in the soil, living cover on soil for more days of the year, fewer chemical inputs, better animal husbandry, and less waste.[17] These multiplying farms of the future will practice regenerative agriculture wherever possible and produce more goods, including energy, carbon sequestration, water filtration and storage; and their caretakers will be learning, measuring, and sharing ecological information.

The Nature Conservancy (TNC) has created an 8,500-acre project on Staten Island, California, that adjusted practices on active farmland to create bird habitat in the Sacramento-San Joaquin River Delta. Over the 20 years since TNC acquired the land in 2001, the organization has been operating a working farm while researching and finetuning wildlife-friendly agriculture and irrigation techniques that promote conservation in an essential habitat for wintering destination for Sandhill Cranes moving along the Pacific Flyway. Funded by grants from the state and federal government, Staten Island demonstrates how wildlife-friendly farming can be economically viable for farmers, while creating a laboratory for science-based approaches to habitat creation in the face of drought and climate change.

Stone House Farm in Livingston, New York, is a 2,000-acre research and demonstration farm that grows and collects data about diverse crops and livestock operations while maintaining 15 permanent carbon research sites. Through its sister nonprofit, Hudson Carbon, the farm is a place-based platform for policy design, exploring the potential of farmers with different crop mixes engaging the NORI carbon market and pushing redesign of New York State's carbon farming program. Stone House Farm and Hudson Carbon have invited outside evaluators from research universities to document the outcomes of their many ongoing experiments to increase the credibility of the research and promote wide adoption of techniques.[18]

Post-agricultural habitat restoration: Designed landscapes have the capacity to help people make sense of boom-and-bust agricultural cycles of production agriculture in growing regions like the lettuce and winter vegetable capital of North America in the contiguous Yuma, Mexicali, and Imperial valleys of the Sonora Desert. In this area, giant laser-leveled tracts of produce are arrayed between barren rock mountains, volcanic cinder cones, dunes, chaparral, and salt lakes. Water is dammed and stored in sublime canyons and conveyed in sleek canals that slice through tan mineral landscapes and direct the water to crop fields where the agricultural utility of soils is nearly spent. In this dramatic context, landscape designer Fred Phillips has created strong precedents for ecological adaptations that are proving the workability of low-cost tactics for renewing post-agricultural waste lands. Phillips's 1,400-acre Yuma East Wetlands (which cost only $9 million to build) retains the legibility of the flood irrigation system, and cultivates different habitat plant community "crops" that make visible growth differentials based on time and water allocation. Phillips engaged the Indigenous Quechan, students, the business community, farmers, and environmentalists in the clearing, cultivation, and maintenance of Yuma East Wetlands – a barn-raising approach to biodiversity that produced lasting engagement and stewardship.

Kinship of Agriculture and Landscape Architecture

Agriculture—the basis first of settlement and then survival once settled— is where landscape architecture began. *History of the Italian Agricultural Landscape* (1961) by Emilio Sereni documents the agricultural history of Italy from antiquity to the 20th century in its cultural and economic context. Sereni analyzes changes that affected Italy's environment over time, and the successes and failures of the design efforts of farmers, engineers, and other technicians in successive generations as they worked to adapt the environment of Italy's different regions for agriculture, responding to the changing climate, variable water and soil conditions, and a range of other challenges.[19] Sereni's work is a foundational text on agriculture, credited with originating the concept of the historical "agricultural landscape" as cultural landscape that encompasses economic and social history, art history and archeology, linguistics, and ecology. From his perspective, Italy didn't emerge as a center of civilization because land and water offered idyllic conditions for agriculture, its people created those conditions with waves of adaptation and landscape architectural innovation that were enmeshed in the design of other aspects of culture and livelihood.

New scholarship about the Americas argues that indigenous civilizations, particularly in present-day Mexico, Peru, and Bolivia, did not live lightly on the land. They had enormous, effective impact on reshaping the land for agricultural enterprise.[20] Most of this scholarship suggests that the so-called New World was very likely the Old World, with several complex civilizations evolving very early through superior plant hybridization and diverse, transformative, region-specific landscape architectures for agriculture and aquaculture (in climates more challenging than those of most early civilizations in Europe and Asia). Indigenous peoples of the Americas invented the plants (maize, most influentially), the symbiotic plant communities, and elaborate new settings—landscape architectures, though not credited as such—in which they could grow. Design of urban cultural and spiritual landscapes followed, developing in parallel with agricultural landscapes far more complex than just fields, with each type referring to, and often embedded, in the others.

In other words, agriculture was core territory of our craft and its mandate long before the term "landscape architecture" was coined or the discipline was recognized. To cede this territory, or work only on its rarified margins, as we have, dissolves the relationship between culture and agriculture as the art of survival most rooted in landscape. If landscape architects are to lay out pathways to policy reform and spatial change in production agriculture, we will need to move away from landscape designs inspired by agriculture or the ornamented farm, evocative as they are, to reach for scale and differences that matter quantitatively and qualitatively. The project examples in this essay establish workable territories for the integration of physical design and policy design. In these examples, evidence-based design helps bridge the two spheres by imagining alternative futures, visualizing the impact of market distortions, illustrating options and tradeoffs between values, supporting public conversation, and especially through physical design that successfully (verifiably) embodies sound systems thinking. In the short term, our focus ought to be on collaborative planning and design of rural landscapes that test, measure, and fine-tune the most effective land-use scenarios for multiple benefits, so that policy and incentives can be better calibrated to induce them. The resulting design output would address perhaps the key challenge of politically engaged landscape architecture in this area: to project credible visions of the collective, and to deploy the craft's centuries of engagement with agriculture to stimulate new appetites.

1. Calculation based on UN Food and Agriculture Organization Data, 2019. See framing of land use issues in Jonathan Foley, "The Other Inconvenient Truth: The Crisis in Global Land Use," *Yale Environment 360* (October 9, 2009).

2. USDA Economic Research Service, http://www.ers.usda.gov/topics/farm-practices-management/irrigation-water-use.aspx.

3. Johan Rockstrom, et al., "A Safe Operating Space for Humanity," *Nature* 461 (2009), 472–75.

4. Hannah Ritchie, "Food production is responsible for one-quarter of the world's greenhouse gas emissions," *Our World in Data* (November 6, 2019), https://ourworldindata.org/food-ghg-emissions.

5. As mechanization and economies of scale depress prices, most farmers own too few acres to make a living. Families who have farmed for generations, including Native American and Canadian nations, and land reform cooperatives in Mexico, now lease their land (and sometimes their water rights) to corporations and contract growers. And because corporations only lease the ground they till, they can deplete and salinate the soils and aquifers, overwork waterways and ecosystems, and move on.

6. Laura Jackson, "Who Designs the Agricultural Landscape," *Landscape Journal* 27 (2008): 1–8.

7. Ibid.

8. Ibid.

9. World Economic Forum, https://www.weforum.org/agenda/2016/12/this-map-shows-how-much-each-country-spends-on-food/.

10. See, e.g., Dana Jackson & Laura Jackson, *The Farm as Natural Habitat: Reconnecting Food Systems with Ecosystems* (Island Press, 2002); George Boody, et al., "Multifunctional Agriculture in the United States," *Bioscience* 55 (2005): 27–38; Joan Nassauer, et al., "The Landscape in 2025: Alternative Landscape Future Scenarios as a Means to Consider Agricultural Policy," *Journal of Soil and Water Conservation* 57, no. 2 (2002); Mary Santelmann, et al., "Assessing Alternative Futures for Agriculture in Iowa" in *Landscape Ecology* 19 (2004): 357–74; Michael Burkhart, et al., "Impacts of Integrated Crop-Livestock Systems on Nitrogen Dynamics and Soil Erosion in Western Iowa Watersheds," *Journal of Geophysical Research-Biogeosciences* 110 (2006).

11. Joan Nassauer, Lecture at the University of Utah, 2016, discussing prior work including, "What Will the Neighbors Think? Cultural Norms and Ecological Design," *Landscape and Urban Planning* 92 (2009).

12. See, e.g., Arnim Wiek & Claudia Binder, "Solutions Spaces for Decision-making: A sustainability assessment tool for city-regions," *Environmental Impact Assessment Review* 25, no. 6 (2005).

13. Richard Buchanan, "Wicked Problems in Design Thinking," *Design Issues* 8, no. 2 (1992), 5–21.

14. Ibid.

15. Highlands Hydroway was developed to the concept level for the Fourth Regional Plan for New York, New Jersey, and Connecticut in a collaboration between Port Urbanism and Architecture and my office.

16. See Kaufman's talk at the Farm of the Future symposium, https://vimeo.com/472775278.

17. I am collaborating with large animal veterinarians Andy Hoffman, dean of the University of Pennsylvania Veterinary School, and Gary Althouse, landscape colleagues Nick Pevzner and Zach Hammaker, and agricultural conservation planner Tom Daniels on this PennPraxis project.

18. See "Farm of the Future" interview at https://vimeo.com/466700636.

19. Marc Bloch did the same for France in *The Original Characteristics of French Rural History* (1931).

20. The new scholarship by archaeologists and scientists is effectively summarized by journalist Charles Mann in *1491: New Revelations of the Americas Before Columbus* (Vintage, 2006). He provides detailed citations of the primary and secondary sources.

WATER

Matthijs Bouw

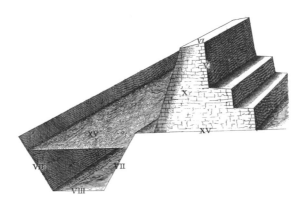

Matthijs Bouw is the Dutch founder of One Architecture and Urbanism (ONE), an Amsterdam- and New York-based design firm. ONE is a global leader in the use of design to conceive and advance climate adaptation and mitigation projects, including Manhattan's coastal protection strategy and many large-scale nature-based solutions projects around the world. He directs the Urban Resilience Certificate Program at the University of Pennsylvania Weitzman School of Design, where he is a professor of practice and the McHarg Center Fellow for Risk and Resilience.

The term resilience has different meanings in different domains. In general, in the engineering world, the term refers to the ability to withstand or bounce back from shocks or stresses.[1] Such simple definitions not only run the risk of overlooking the distinctions between damage mitigation, resilience, and adaptation, they also misrepresent the transformative potential of the concept. The use of the more complex definition of (urban) resilience, as the "capacity of individuals, communities, institutions, business, and systems within a city to survive, adapt, and grow no matter what kinds of chronic stresses and acute shocks they experience,"[2] as the organization 100 Resilient Cities popularized it, challenges us to think of our urban systems as complex and adaptive. It also encourages us to learn to work at different scales simultaneously in the social and the physical domain, and accept and embrace emergence and uncertainty.

From this resilience lens, nature-based solutions have become increasingly important as tools for climate-responsive design because rather than subjecting nature to the folly of control, they harness the forces of nature to generate societal benefits. In the past decades, coastal wetlands and foreshores have been restored, for instance, because they not only attenuate wave action, they also promote biodiversity, store carbon, and have recreational benefits. In projects such as the Building with Nature project in Demak, Indonesia, the growth of mangroves has been promoted because they also act as nurseries for fish and crustaceans, capture sediment and keep it in place, and improve the economy of the local communities. Mangrove belts not only prevent coastal erosion but allow the coast to grow in the face of sea level rise. The Sand Motor project in the Netherlands distributes sand along the coast using the ocean's current, fortifying the coast with a less frequent, and therefore a less disruptive, dredging regimen.[3] These solutions emulate the coastal dynamics that we see in nature and are very different from earlier coastal projects that typically used bulkheads, levees, and groins to keep things in place while themselves disturbing natural flows. There are many examples of hard engineered coastal protection systems that, while providing (temporary) relief from coastal flooding and erosion, disturb the coastal dynamics by increasing erosion elsewhere. Such protection can also starve other areas from the sediment needed to sustain the coast and keep the beaches from drowning by denying the inherent dynamics of coastal systems, where beaches, dunes, and marshes are constantly migrating.

The definition that IUCN, the International Union for Conservation of Nature, gives to nature-based solutions—"actions to protect, sustainably manage, and restore natural or modified ecosystems, that address societal challenges effectively and adaptively, simultaneously providing human well-being and biodiversity benefits"[4]—acknowledges that conservation per se is not where nature-based solutions will lead us, especially in the United States. There is simply too little to conserve on the waterfronts of the American City, and the impacts of the climate crisis will be such that what little there is will be drowned anyway because the systems that sustain natural resources have been too severely interrupted. Because doubling down on the rigid and constructed coastline will eventually reach its limits, and will be too costly for many areas, the only truly resilient approach for our coastal cities is a landscape project in which gray infrastructure solutions slowly give way to nature-based solutions at scale, combined with managed retreat. These solutions will provide ecosystem services and, above all, buffer and absorb the shocks of rapid environmental change. Such a landscape project is partly restorative (also in terms of environmental justice) and partly forward looking. It will need to reimagine the infrastructures that sustain our communities and deal with a radically different climate. Reclaiming the old, undoing layers of infrastructure, and innovating with nature brings an entirely new paradigm to design, at a radically different scale and timescale.

In the Northeastern US, we already see increased tidal (sunny day) flooding. Sea level rise is expected to be between 1.5 and 3 feet by mid-century, and between 3 and 6 feet by late century (although a rapid Antarctic melt scenario could bring, according to some scientists, as much as 10 feet).[5] If the climate crisis continues apace, and the ice masses of Greenland and Antarctica continue to melt, we are looking at more than 100 feet in the centuries that follow. This means that not only the low-lying areas in our coastal cities will start to flood, but also, as upland streams (or sewers) will not be able to release their water, inland flooding will increase.

The magnitude of the transformation of our urban systems that this will eventually require is difficult to imagine, but a number of things seem inevitable. We will need to restore our natural systems at scale and design them such that they can adapt to a changing climate and provide ecosystem benefits. We will need to start a process of managed retreat from flood-prone areas, first from areas of low density (which, in the American model of binary cities, with small high-density downtowns and extensive single-family suburbs, are dominant), but eventually also from those areas that we are now designing flood protection systems for, and clean up the mess in the process. We need to find space in our urban areas to store stormwater. We need to design our infrastructure in a more flexible and decentralized way, using, when possible, natural infrastructure, taking into account other climate change impacts such as increased temperatures and longer periods of drought. And we need to engage our communities so that this process—which must start now and will take centuries—is equitable and just, offering local agency while building local stewardship. Everywhere, but particularly coastal areas, will need "Adaptive Management Strategies" to curate the complex interactions within ecosystems and between ecosystems and humans.

This landscape project presents an enormous opportunity for landscape architecture to fulfill its McHargian mandate in the 21st century (and beyond). In the early phases, we will have to continue to implement a wide variety of pilot projects, so that we can learn to work through the myriad challenges and engage stakeholders and communities. Nature-based solutions can play a role in reconnecting communities to the water, remediating toxic sites, cleaning our water and wastewater, reducing the impacts of waves, storing carbon, and increasing biodiversity while improving physical and mental health outcomes and cooling our cities. Such pilot projects will help us understand the possibilities of designing with nature, help make the case for them, and build stewardship. Of course, such projects will, in the next decades, be accompanied by a suite of measures to protect critical infrastructure and high-density urban areas, while simultaneously decentralizing our infrastructures and moving them away from risky areas.

Because the expected lifespan of our infrastructures is long, and any investment in infrastructure needs to consider the radically different climate reality during its entire lifespan, as well as that of its interconnected parts, it is imperative to start changing the land-use patterns and infrastructure investments such that future risks are avoided. In the process, the space we preserve by stopping development in areas with long-term risk, and the space we gain by migrating away from them, through processes of managed retreat and the removal of the highways, power plants, and waste infrastructure within these risk zones will slowly grow. This will allow pilot projects to be built out at the scale needed to perform ecosystem services on a scale commensurate with the crisis.

Getting the theory of the resilience project right is, however, the easy part. Retrofitting our cities with viable long-term resilience projects in practice is difficult. Working in the American city since the aftermath of Superstorm Sandy, I have come to understand just how far the American city has developed in a relatively short time span, treating the ancestral lands of the First Nations as virgin nature that could be dominated through fossil-fuel driven technologies, supported by extractive economies and compliant regulations. This is most visible in the waterfronts, where, starting in the 19th but accelerating from the 20th century, marshes and wetlands have been filled, often with trash and pollutants, in order to unlock real estate "value" or provide a tabula rasa for infrastructure and industry. Mixed in with the mechanics of American cities are, however, real communities, often poor and of color, often there because of the proximity to work, and the affordability of the locations, and sometimes forced there by design, through redlining or availability of public housing. In a vicious cycle, these communities have then endured environmental pollution as well as sustained disinvestment.

Much of this development has been driven by a mix of hubris and greed by the private sector, with a modicum of government intervention to stamp out corruption and conserve whatever might be left of nature or history. America's veneration of entrepreneurship and individual responsibility, however, has shaped an environment in which the taking of economic risk is encouraged, where externalities are not considered, and where catastrophic risk, created by hazards such as hurricanes, floods, and now rising sea levels is accepted as an incidental consequence of liberty. And until recently, the combination of grift, racism, corruption, extraction, and myths of individual responsibility has worked pretty well for many.

But in the past centuries, the earth's climate has been relatively stable. This meant that risk from flooding and hurricanes, for instance, fell well within a predictable and manageable bandwidth, and that the safety margins built into the city were sufficient to prevent social chaos in the face of such disasters. The climate crisis changes all that. The stability of earth's climate system has given way to "global weirding," where weather-related events become increasingly unpredictable. The "stationarity myth," as Katharine Hayhoe calls it, has exploded.[6] Sea levels and temperatures are rising at an uncertain but accelerating pace, quickly eating up the urban safety margins. If the average New York City bulkhead is 6 feet, the possible 3-foot sea level rise in 50 years means that a storm surge event of half the flood levels of what is now safe will create coastal flooding.

While it is clear that the climate crisis requires significant physical adaptation of our cities (as well as much stronger efforts for the mitigation of greenhouse gas emissions), and that designers can play a huge role in that, it is important to understand that the American city is built upon a set of values and institutions that will need to change if these cities are going to cope with the climate crisis at the scale necessary. Part of that change needs to come through the political domain. But another part will need to come from working through the intersections of the physical (hard) infrastructure and the social (soft) infrastructure, always appraising them as intertwined. The climate crisis poses a set of radically new challenges for which we need to build the culture, the expertise, and the "muscle" to get things done. The magnitude of the climate crisis is such that we have no time to lose and cannot afford to not try many things simultaneously. Learning what works, and what does not, will help direct our political struggles and provide proof of concept for the necessary cultural change.

Our team's design for the Big U, a vision for a protective system that encircles Lower Manhattan, was directly informed by the cultural and institutional reality of American city-making.[7] On many levels, the design is innovative and brings a new understanding of how to design for a changing climate. At the same time, the constraints that the current context imposes has resulted in a project in which the imperative for implementation within the congressional allocated timeframe has required compromises. And, as the original vision is now being implemented, with the first compartment, the East Side Coastal Resiliency project, under construction and six of the other compartments in planning or design, the "lessons learned" from this first series of large-scale coastal adaptation projects in the US help us navigate a path forward.

The design competition from which the Big U vision was born was organized by Rebuild by Design, a not-for-profit primarily funded by the Rockefeller Foundation, with the aim of rethinking how to respond to disasters. The American acceptance of risk and preference for market-driven responses has typically made disaster response a function of the insurance industry. This has resulted in the most vulnerable being caught in a cycle of being unprepared for, and unable to rebuild after, disaster events. Rebuild by Design proposed a more integrated and preventative approach, one centered around communities and their needs, rather than institutions and their methods. This approach revealed the imperative to design for multiple benefits, with the aim to undo some of the inequities that the American city has produced, and that the climate crisis will only exacerbate. In the Big U visioning process, for example, we learned from the community on the Lower East Side about the desire to make East River Park more accessible and useful for the locals, and translated that into the design of a bridging berm. We used the elevation required for flood protection to serve as a bridgehead for new bridges across the Franklin D. Roosevelt East River Drive that separates the park from the housing and redesigned the park to have more passive open space.

An obvious complement to any flood protection system would be to also deploy a nature-based solution such as a "soft shoreline." This would absorb wave energy and provide other ecosystem services but it would also require additional space in-water. Environmental regulations in the US, mostly formulated in the 1970s, limit and challenge any type of new construction in the water. This means that it is very difficult to get permission for such projects, and it would likely take more time than available within congressional spending deadlines. In addition to permit and spatial requirements, the other impediment is that the short- and long-term performance of nature-based approaches is still largely untested and unverifiable. For city agencies, which are averse to innovation at the best of times, trialing a new approach on such a prominent site was a bridge too far. For these reasons the Big-U is initially being built entirely on land, and nature-based solutions

involving the intertidal zone are retained as future components of a longer-term adaptive strategy.

As designers, we were aware how the congressionally mandated 2050 flood levels we planned for would make the initial iteration of the project sound from a cost-benefit analysis. Viewed from the perspective of the long-term change in our climate and sea levels, which will roll out over centuries, it can be considered as a temporary solution that buys us time to learn about these new circumstances and build up institutional knowledge and community trust.

Taken seriously, the landscape project of resilience requires us to reimagine the American city, or actually the American conurbation, with its small downtowns and extensive, mostly single-family developments mixed with infrastructure and low-rise commerce, stretching hundreds of miles from those centers. In what is called the 30 x 30 initiative, President Biden has pledged to conserve 30% of the United States federal land and 30% of its oceans. Currently approximately 12% of the US land is protected.[8] In order to preserve a diversity of ecosystems, it is critical to make sure that the other 18% necessary includes now urbanized areas such as the Eastern seaboard and the Gulf Coast, as well as the various river valleys. From a long-term climate change perspective, this is only logical if not inevitable.

Such a landscape project intersects at all levels and radically transforms the American city, which will necessarily change the dominant paradigm from preservation to designing, engineering, and building with nature. It will help us reinvent the American city as more just and equitable because the project is, by its very definition, a public project. It is a project that requires a new vision of, and by, our communities based upon the realization that the American myth of individual freedom brings tragedy to the commons, that all things are delicately interconnected, and that the climate crisis and its intersections with issues of race, power, and health forces us to choose between eco-fascism where only those who can afford it isolate themselves from its impacts and eco-cosmopolitanism.[9] And while such a project benefits from leadership and a clear vision and articulation of values and top-down policies, it is on-the-ground design that will make the physical transformations with the degree of specificity they will require. Design interventions help communicate the challenges to various actors and stakeholders, propose ways to integrate systems and objectives, and put projects on the road to implementation. Only through a reciprocity between design on the ground and our scientific, financial, and political institutions can we marshal the forces and acquire the knowledge required to create this landscape project.

1. Patrick Martin-Breen & J. Marty Anderies, *Resilience: A Literature Review* (Rockefeller Foundation, 2011).

2. "What is Resilience?" http://resiliencetools.net/node/14.

3. For more information on these projects, see Matthijs Bouw & Erik van Eekelen (eds), *Building with Nature: Creating, Implementing and Scaling Nature-based Solutions* (NAi010publishers, 2020).

4. IUCN, "Nature-based Solutions," https://www.iucn.org/theme/nature-based-solutions.

5. John Englander, *Moving to Higher Ground, Rising Sea Level and the Path Forward* (Science Bookshelf, 2021), ch. 2.

6. Katharina Hayhoe, "The Stationarity Myth: How A Changing Climate Alters the Paradigms of Infrastructure Design and Maintenance" in Aman Khan & Klaus Becker (eds), *US Infrastructure: Challenges and Directions for the 21st Century* (Routledge, 2019).

7. The team consisted of BIG (Bjarke Ingels Group) and One Architecture, with Starr Whitehouse, James Lima Planning + Development, Project Projects, Green Shield Ecology, AEA Consulting, Level Agency for Infrastructure, and Arcadis.

8. Benji Jones, "The Biden Administration has a Game-Changing Approach to Nature Conservation" (May 7, 2021), https://www.vox.com/2021/5/7/22423139/biden-30-by-30-conservation-initiative-historic.

9. Ulrich Beck, "Living in the World Risk Society," *Economy and Society* 35, no. 3 (2006).

ENERGY

Nicholas Pevzner

Nicholas Pevzner is an assistant professor in the Department of Landscape Architecture at the University of Pennsylvania Weitzman School of Design, and a faculty fellow at the Kleinman Center for Energy Policy. His research focuses on the socio-spatial impact of energy infrastructure, including spatial planning for the renewable energy transition. He teaches design studios and courses on urban ecology, the history of energy systems and negative emissions, and on historical lineages of the Green New Deal.

B eyond the scope of design alone, humanity today finds itself in varying stages of a global energy transition – from the fossil-fuel-powered systems and machines of the Industrial Age toward some theoretically decarbonized, net-zero future state. This transformation is expansive and will affect everything from physical infrastructures to social and economic policy and geopolitical relations. We are still early within the larger arc of the global energy transition, with some countries and actors resisting change and others embracing the decarbonization challenge – yet it is plain that the transformation is happening too slowly. Global emissions are rising, and the early symptoms of climate change are already wreaking havoc with worse impacts sure to come.

What is the role of design in relation to the energy transition? Broadly speaking, design can either continue to reify the status quo, or it can push for emerging low-carbon alternatives, and do so within the framework of a "Just Transition."[1] Beyond merely rejecting the inequitable and unsustainable state of the world today, design has to offer specific new narratives for the process of transition as a long-term continuous project of reimagining the post-carbon society. As political theorist Damian White has written, "The day after the demonstration, a just post-carbon world that actively improves people's lives still has to be imagined and built, fabricated and realized, institutionalized and sustained by public support and ongoing engagement. Decarbonizing, decolonizing, democratizing, and decommodifying our carbon-intensive material world is going to require…enormous amounts of creative labor and inventive praxis to build public institutions, a public ecology and a public culture to allow us to survive and flourish on a warming planet."[2] Imagining what exactly constitutes the outcomes of a Just Transition is a major multigenerational design project, and energy systems are central to this much larger set of societal transformations. Because energy systems play out across all forms of landscape and because the discipline of landscape architecture is deeply invested in designing and planning in a way that is attuned to the complex interconnections between social, natural, and technological systems, it is well positioned to help mediate the transition to low-carbon energy systems.

Energy systems are a major driver of climate change, and at the same time one of the sectors furthest along the S-curve of transition – well ahead of trucking, aviation, agriculture, and steel or cement production, for example.[3] Low-carbon alternatives to fossil-fueled energy generation have been in development for a good half-century, with bursts of innovation and deployment over the last two decades that have finally begun to result in cost-competitive low-carbon energy technologies like wind turbines and solar photovoltaics, which we can expect to become cheaper still as their economies of scale continue to grow. The scale of deployment for these new low-carbon energy systems will need to be massive as well, to reach internationally agreed-upon decarbonization goals: in the United States, renewable energy deployment will need to triple or quadruple within the current decade – and then keep growing, with wind energy's installed capacity needing to become between six and 28 times larger than today's, and solar energy's between nine and 39 times larger to reach net-zero emissions by 2050, according to a recent "Net-Zero America" study from Princeton University.[4]

These changes will require a lot of land. To generate the clean energy for a grid that has electrified its transportation and buildings sectors, the Princeton study found that at least 228,000 square miles will be needed by 2050 within the US for onshore wind and solar farms.[5] Clearly, the energy transition is a transformation that will not simply switch out one type of power plant for another, but one that will fundamentally reshape the geography of energy generation, and that will come with dramatic impacts in terms of the space needed, as well as impacts to land use, and to landscapes. Landscape architecture, largely missing from the energy conversation so far, is well-poised to play a much more important role in mediating how this massive buildout of clean energy systems lands in specific places and specific communities, and how these communities perceive such a drastic transformation.

A Socio-spatial Question

Questions of energy infrastructure are most often considered through the lens of financing or technological constraints. But while these things are vitally important to successful energy transitions, they leave out the questions of space and its cultural considerations – a critical omission, considering that the energy transitions at their core are socio-spatial problems. As geographers like Gavin Bridge have noted, "energy systems are constituted spatially: the components of the systems are embedded in particular settings and the networked nature of the system itself produces geographies of connection, dependency, and control."[6] Bridge and his coauthors define *energy landscapes* as constituting "the constellation of activities and socio-technical linkages associated with energy capture, conversion, distribution, and consumption." In terms of specific spatial patterns or organizations within the energy landscape, they offer examples such as "the classic 'choke point' and 'bottleneck' geographies associated with the international shipment of crude oil or the management of electricity distribution grids."[7] And yet, as they explain, "it is the temporal concept of 'transition'—rather than a geographical alternative—that is most often mobilised for thinking about the changes involved in developing low-carbon energy systems."[8]

Landscapes, of course, are not the same thing as mere space. As Dutch landscape architect Dirk Sijmons has written, "landscape is a rich and layered concept that speaks as much to the relationship between humans and nature as it does to the relationship between people themselves. Landscape is loaded with values, from individual memories to social symbols."[9] And while it's true that the energy transition will require a lot of space, it's even more challenging to think about the socio-spatial transformations that will be required to so many, often beloved, landscapes around the world.

As Sijmons and environmental designer Machiel van Dorst have noted, "space and its sociopolitical arena" is where all these factors come together; this "will be the battlefield where the energy transition will be won or lost."[10] In fact it is precisely the cultural and socio-political factors tied to landscape, such as the possibility of community opposition to the visual and land-use impacts of wind, solar, and transmission projects, that represent the most likely bottlenecks to renewable energy deployment at the speed and scale that are necessary.[11] Landscape, in other words, is an important site of contestation for the deployment of clean energy, and the energy transition is as much a socio-spatial problem as a political or economic one. Part of what is needed, beyond just engineering, law, and finance, is a strong cultural case for landscape transformation, that incorporates a socio-spatial approach to the patterns of energy generation and transmission, energy use, and urban form.

Machines in the Garden

Energy technology, much like the earlier factories of the Industrial Age, has routinely been theorized as an unnatural and alien imposition upon wild, pastoral, or scenic landscapes.[12] Landscape architects' engagement with energy technology has often revolved around finding ways to reduce the perceived visual impacts of its intrusion.[13] As landscape architect Gary Strang has noted, "[d]esigners have most often been charged with hiding, screening and cosmetically mitigating infrastructure, in order to maintain the image of the untouched natural surroundings of an earlier era. They are rarely asked to consider infrastructure as an opportunity, as a fundamental and regional form."[14] Strang, writing in *Places Journal* 25 years ago, proposed instead that infrastructures (from water conveyance and water treatment systems to power lines to communication lines to oil, steam, and natural gas lines) should be recognized as critical functional layers of the contemporary landscape, and given "a formal clarity that expresses their importance to society, at the same time creating new layers of urban landmarks, spaces and connections."[15] Yet in the intervening years little design integration has taken place, at least in the United States, and the continuing resistance of many people to new energy infrastructures in their backyards has fed myriad instances of local opposition to new solar farms and wind farms, as well as new and upgraded high-voltage transmission lines – all necessary components of a low-carbon energy system. The result has been to drag out the approvals process for years, often killing the projects outright or through delay and litigation.[16]

Instead of seeing energy infrastructure as a blight on the landscape, and something that must be covered up or kept far away, might designers be employed instead in reframing this infrastructure as a positive landscape addition – as a beneficial new layer to the existing cultural landscape that can create a positive new landscape experience despite its close proximity to observers and visitors?[17] We can look to smaller European countries that have dedicated more design attention to the configuration of renewable energy landscapes, such as Denmark and the Netherlands, for examples of better spatial integration of energy infrastructure into the landscape, with earlier and more sustained engagement from landscape architects, that result in more carefully designed energy landscapes, which in turn receive a more positive reception. In a Dutch example, Sijmons and his design firm H+N+S Landscape Architects evaluated an existing energy landscape, full of ad hoc and solitary wind turbines of numerous makes, models, heights, and colors, that had been added over time in the Wieringermeer polder since the 1970s as part of a municipal spatial quality plan for wind energy. H+N+S developed clear rules for

reorganizing the layout of the wind farm through placement of new turbines and some selective removals of old ones, and carefully curated the way in which visitors encounter the turbines as they traverse the landscape.

The Danish government routinely hires landscape architecture firms as consultants to review the proposed siting of wind turbines in the landscape, and to develop proactive plans for renewable infrastructure. Municipalities are responsible for designating areas that are suitable for wind development, through a municipal planning process that "gives full consideration to neighboring residences, nature, the landscape, cultural-historical values, etc., and of course the possibility of harvesting the wind resource."[18] The early involvement of landscape architects and planners in the energy planning process not only allows for the creation of a positive image for renewable energy, but it also allows them the opportunity to holistically analyze, and then by design mitigate various foreseeable negative impacts on local community landscapes and local ecosystems.

This approach is intended to prevent the kind of monofunctional, out-of-scale, brutalist energy development that characterized the United States' early experience with renewable energy, in places like Tehachapi Pass in California, which have become known pejoratively in other countries as "wind walls."[19] California was an early adopter of renewable technologies, and initially opted for a hands-off approach to energy development, resulting in examples like Tehachapi, with hundreds of wind turbines cacophonously arranged at various heights and elevations, composed of numerous turbine makes and models, all spinning at different speeds and in different directions; in short, a total absence of design. Similarly, early California solar thermal and solar photovoltaic projects have led to numerous so-called "green on green" battles[20] over land use between different environmental groups because of their impacts to sensitive desert habitats and the privatization of public landscapes.

California since then has embraced a degree of spatial planning in its energy-siting procedures, such as with its Desert Renewable Energy Conservation Plan (DRECP), Renewable Energy Transmission Initiative (RETI), and Competitive Renewable Energy Zones (CREZs) – all regional-scale landscape planning approaches that attempt to balance the concerns of competing renewable energy and conservation stakeholders, all employing explicitly spatial methods that pay attention to geographically specific considerations. However, even with these frameworks, while some degree of public input and participation is achieved, and large landscapes are appraised from a geospatial perspective, designers are not directly involved in siting the energy infrastructures, nor are any specific strategies employed for thinking through how the public might engage with these new energy landscapes at close range, or what additional functions these energy-scapes could include.

The Technological Sublime

The renewable energy transition is not the first time that the "technological object" of an energy regime has "collided head-on," to quote energy historian David E. Nye, "with the quintessential object of the natural sublime."[21] Nye cites prior confrontations, such as when the hydroelectric-powered factory usurped the waters of Niagara Falls, or when the Hoover Dam confronted the Colorado River canyons of the desert Southwest. In each of those cases, the technological object itself took on qualities of the sublime, drawing visitors and onlookers, who used language very similar to that of sublime natural landscapes—awe and grandeur—to describe their feelings, but evoked here by the scale and power of these feats of engineering.[22]

During the 1930s New Deal of the Roosevelt Administration, the design of energy infrastructure took advantage of these emotions, using architecture and landscape design to craft gleaming visions of modernity and progress amid the desolation of the Great Depression.[23] The planners of the big Colorado River dams and of the early TVA dams understood and manipulated these emotions, celebrating the confrontation with natural landscapes and using design as an intermediary. The visitor's experience of the dams was meticulously choreographed to evoke wonderment, optimism, and pride: from the carefully crafted cinematic approach road to the final scene of monolithic form, everything was curated to overwhelm the visitor with what Nye has called the "technological sublime." Visitor centers told the story of the multipurpose system of infrastructures, playing up the improvements to good land stewardship and economic benefit using architecture, interpretive material, and signage. Rather than relying on arguments of efficiency and functionality, these infrastructures were examples of the power of civic persuasion.[24]

Is this concept of the technological sublime still relevant in the context of renewable energy, or are we in a fundamentally different paradigm, with increasingly decentralized energy rendering energy landscapes essentially invisible? Certainly with some technologies, such as rooftop solar, the energy system does retreat from a highly visible element in the landscape toward ever-closer integration with architectural building systems. But the scale of the decarbonization challenge facing the world is such that for the next several decades, at the very least, there will be need for a lot of extremely visible renewable energy landscapes, from large-scale solar arrays and ever-larger wind turbines onshore and offshore, to newer energy technologies, such as energy storage and carbon capture facilities. Can a closeness with the unfamiliar technological object of the new clean energy regime help to coalesce a stronger consensus around the energy transition? Projects such as Walter Hood Studio's *Solar Strand* at the University at Buffalo are rare examples of solar arrays that are designed around public access, with visitors free to stroll through the 5,000-photovoltaic panel array along open paths, amid biodiverse meadow plantings. While this project is an expensive one-off, it does point the way toward close coordination between designer and energy developer, with the role of the public carefully considered in an energy project's spatial experience.

Emerging Energy Landscapes

While wind and solar energy dominate the discussion of the renewable energy future today, several other forms of energy technologies are emerging and will need to find places within the physical landscapes of the future energy regime. Energy storage is an important component of renewable energy systems for its role in helping to stabilize the grid and balance out naturally occurring fluctuations in wind or solar production, resulting in so-called "firmed" renewable energy. A well-developed technology for energy storage, pumped-storage hydro, is similar in many ways to traditional hydroelectric dams, albeit able to run in reverse and pump water in both directions. Some examples of public pumped storage landscapes with high public access exist within the TVA system, notably the Raccoon Mountain Pumped-Storage hydroelectric facility outside of Chattanooga, Tennessee, which features public hiking and mountain biking trails, a well-designed visitor center, and a dramatic overlook to the city and river gorge below. Similar pumped-storage landscapes have been proposed, and some built, on former quarries and abandoned mines, sometimes rebranded "quarry batteries" – a potentially beneficial multipurpose energy landscape typology that deserves much more design attention.[25]

Increasingly, lithium ion batteries are overshadowing pumped-storage hydro as the energy storage technology of choice, and the full range of design implications of such lithium ion projects are not yet well understood. Batteries can be placed in standard-looking shipping containers or camouflaged to look like typical buildings. Yet, as more US states push ahead with mandatory energy storage requirements, more battery installations are taking place outdoors, in battery banks that replicate in many ways the spatial patterns of solar projects, substations, and other elements of the energy grid. But here too, multi-purpose approaches to energy storage alongside other public uses can increase public benefits and integrate projects better into their landscape.

Yet other energy storage technologies are emerging, with other chemistries and with untested opportunities for design integration. Electric vehicles and their charging infrastructure are poised to reconfigure many established logics of the transportation system and the public right-of-way. And as carbon capture technology continues to be developed, tested, and deployed, we face another round of contestation over the role and impact of carbon capture and storage facilities, CO_2 pipelines, CO_2 tanker ports, geologic storage CO_2 injection wells, and other components of a carbon management infrastructural system that mimics in many ways the very fossil-fuel-powered energy systems whose emissions it is intended to counteract. The scale, organization, and ownership model of these energy systems is neither neutral nor uncontested, with large corporations and utilities (including some of the same companies that are responsible for the bulk of historic CO_2 emissions) pushing aggressively to build and control the new low-carbon infrastructures of the post-carbon future, and community organizations and climate justice advocates pushing back in favor of local control, local accountability, local energy ownership, equitable energy access, and decent access to energy jobs – arrangements known broadly as energy democracy.[26] The role of design in communicating the role and public benefit of these new energy landscapes for climate stabilization and grid stability will be more important than ever to make clear the complex interconnections between social, natural, and technological systems, make legible the connections to the energy that is more and more central to people's everyday lives, and to mitigate to some degree the inevitable pushback against necessary transformations—large and small—in people's backyards. Designers must be mindful to understand the lines of conflict, and the political implications of energy infrastructure, so that they help accelerate the low-carbon energy transition without unwittingly reinforcing patterns of inequality and exploitation.

We've now had several energy transitions in the history of the world: from muscle to wood to water to coal to oil and now the transition to renewables. Each new energy transition has unleashed the exploitation of new territories – landscapes of extraction that supply the inputs that keep the system running. Energy transitions are political, and they proceed unevenly across the landscape, empowering some places and bypassing others, while leaving certain places with the toxic legacies of extraction. Today we are on the cusp of a new energy transition, but it too will not be neutral, nor uncontested. It too opens up potential new territories of extraction: lithium mining in South America and cobalt in the Congo for batteries and renewable technologies,[27] large-scale renewable energy projects that steamroll local communities and extract profit.[28] How might designers think of their role as territorial and political agents in this moment of rapid energy transition, operating on the energy landscape and mindful of the associated landscapes of extraction?

With the most recent efforts of the US federal government in funding a newfound push on infrastructure investment, there is once again an opportunity, as in the 1930s New Deal era, for the active participation of designers in the energy space to help ensure that this new generation of low-carbon infrastructure avoids hastily considered top-down siting policies that might result in local opposition and resistance, and to help achieve careful and site-sensitive siting outcomes. There are some basic principles that designers can incorporate, such as a focus on multifunctionality and the sharing of land uses; on proactive public engagement; on site-appropriate scale, alignment, and rhythm; a careful detailing of the edges where the majority of public interactions occur; consideration of visitor experience; and attention to the effect of energy systems on labor and on demands for energy democracy.[29]

But first, designers need to be included in the energy planning process early enough to make a difference in the siting and design of energy projects. As in the 1930s, landscape architects are needed within government agencies and within utilities and energy companies from where they can proactively reach out to local municipalities to help improve their local energy planning. They are needed in the by-lines of journal articles and op-eds, on TV and radio, and in public hearings to advocate and lobby for good public policy, and to help steer the public discussion. And their collective efforts on thousands of individual projects are needed to imagine and build and give form to a diversity of inspiring new just and multifunctional energy landscapes. The transformations of the low-carbon energy transition will touch virtually every corner of the physical environment, and landscape architects must not only be ready to work with this unfamiliar yet ubiquitous medium, but to uncork the bottlenecks of opposition and the chokepoints of deployment of this new energy regime – to help accelerate the energy transition and bring a fairer, more just, more resilient, and more livable post-carbon future into being.

1. The Just Transition framework has several lineages, and the term has been in use since the 1980s by trade unions and climate justice groups, originally to diffuse labor-versus-environmentalist tensions. At their core its general principles highlight a focus on just outcomes for communities that stand to face disproportionate harm from climate change —most often low-income communities and communities of color— as well as workers that stand to be economically impacted by the transition away from fossil energy. See, Peter Newell & Dustin Mulvaney, "The Political Economy of the Just Transition," *The Geographical Journal* 179, no. 2 (2013): 132–40.

2. Damian White, "Just Transitions/Design for Transitions: Preliminary Notes on a Design Politics for a Green New Deal," *Capitalism Nature Socialism* 31, no. 2 (2020): 17.

3. Danny Cullenward & David G. Victor, *Making Climate Policy Work* (Polity Press, 2020), 4–5.

4. Eric Larson et al., "Net-Zero America: Potential Pathways, Infrastructure, and Impacts," interim report (Princeton University, December 15, 2020), 90.

5. Ibid., 172.

6. Gavin Bridge, et al., "Geographies of Energy Transition: Space, place, and the low-carbon economy," *Energy Policy* 53 (2013): 333.

7. Ibid.

8. Ibid.

9. Dirk Sijmons et al., (eds), *Landscape and Energy: Designing Transition* (nai010 Publishers, 2014), 12.

10. Dirk Sijmons & Machiel van Dorst, "Strong Feelings: Emotional landscape of wind turbines," in Sven Stremke & Andy Van den Dobbelsteen (eds), *Sustainable Energy Landscapes: Designing, Planning, and Development* (CRC Press/Taylor & Francis, 2012), 46.

11. Multiple recent studies have identified land use conflict as one of the likeliest bottlenecks: Larson et al., "New-Zero America," 334; Samantha Gross, "Renewables, Land Use, and Local Opposition in the United States" (Brookings Institution, January 2020), 1–2.

12. Leo Marx has documented the impact that factories and steam power produced on the pastoral idea in American cultural life throughout the 19th century, and David Nye has unpacked the aesthetic impact of the factory on the idea of sublime landscape. See, Leo Marx, *Machine in the Garden: Technology and the Pastoral idea in America* (Oxford University Press, 2000); David E. Nye, *American Technological Sublime* (The MIT Press, 1994), 109–42.

13. Dean Apostol et al., *The Renewable Energy Landscape: Preserving scenic values in our sustainable energy future* (Routledge, 2017).

14. Gary L. Strang, "Infrastructure as Landscape, Landscape as Infrastructure," *Places* 10, no. 3 (1996): 11.

15. Ibid., 10.

16. Among notable recent US examples of low-carbon energy infrastructures that have failed because of scenic or habitat conservation concerns, are the Cape Wind offshore wind farm in Nantucket Sound, the Battle Born Solar project in Nevada, and the Northern Pass high-voltage transmission line in New Hampshire. Farmers have also increasingly started to voice opposition to large-scale solar development on agriculture land in some states.

17. Hanna K. Szumilas-Kowalczyk & Nicholas Pevzner, "Getting Beyond Visual Impact: Designing Renewable Energy as a Positive Landscape Addition," Visual Resource Stewardship Conference (2019), https://digitalcommons.esf.edu/vrconference/11.

18. Danish Ministry of Environment and Food – Nature Agency, "Store vindmøller i det åbne land [Large wind turbines in the open country]," 2007, http://naturstyrelsen.dk/publikationer/2007/jan/store-vindmoeller-i-det-aabne-land/.

19. Craig Morris & Arne Jungjohan, *Energy Democracy: Germany's Energiewende to Renewables* (Palgrave Macmillan, 2016), 61.

20. Dustin Mulvaney, "Identifying the Roots of Green Civil War Over Utility-scale Solar

Energy Projects on Public Lands Across the American Southwest," *Journal of Land Use Science* 12, no. 6 (2017): 49–515.

21. Nye, *American Technological Sublime*, 137.

22. Ibid., 136–37, 140.

23. Walter L. Creese, *TVA's Public Planning: The Vision, the Reality* (The University of Tennessee Press, 1990), 1–3.

24. Jane Wolff, "Redefining Landscape," in Tim Culvahouse (ed.), *The Tennesse Valley Authority: Design and Persuasion* (Princeton Architectural Press, 2007), 56–57.

25. For speculative visions of pumped-storage hydro projects, see Nicholas Pevzner, "Landscape, Public Imagination, and the Green New Deal," *Landscape Architecture Magazine* (July 2019). For built examples of this kind of brownfield reuse, one example is the Kidson 250MW Pumped Storage Hydro Project, Queensland, Australia, on the site of a former gold mine.

26. Climate Justice Alliance, "Energy Democracy - Climate Justice Alliance," https://climatejusticealliance.org/workgroup/energy-democracy/.

27. Thea Riofrancos, "Seize and Resist," *The Baffler* 54 (November 2020), https://thebaffler.com/salvos/seize-and-resist-riofrancos.

28. For good descriptions of exploitative arrangements of some renewable energy systems and actors, as well as of exploitative fossil fuel systems and actors, see: Shalonda H. Baker, *Revolutionary Power: An Activist's Guide to the Energy Transition* (Island Press, 2021).

29. Nicholas Pevzner, Yekang Ko & Kirk Dimond, "Power Player: Designing for Just and Multifunctional Energy Landscapes," *Landscape Architecture Magazine* (June 2021).

PUBLIC

Christopher Marcinkoski

Christopher Marcinkoski is a licensed architect and associate professor of landscape architecture and urban design at the University of Pennsylvania Weitzman School of Design. He is a founding partner of PORT, a Philadelphia- and Chicago-based public realm and urban design practice recognized with the Architectural League of New York's 2020 Emerging Voices award. Christopher is the author of *The City That Never Was* (2016), and guest editor of *LA+ SPECULATION* (2022). He is a fellow of the American Academy in Rome.

P rior to the events of 2020, making an argument for the value of critically considering real (as opposed to digital) social interactions in actual (physical) public spaces likely would have seemed nostalgic, at best, or intellectually retrograde, at worst. The findings of Holly Whyte, Jan Gehl, and others remain well known, but within contemporary landscape architecture discourse and studio pedagogy today—at least in the United States—consideration of the importance of the urban public realm has often been seen as a given and not something particularly worthy of active, critical inquiry.[1] *Public space is good, sure. Everyone likes parks and piazzas, yeah. Projects like X or Y are compelling, without a doubt.* But frankly, that is kind of it. Within leading American schools of landscape architecture, physically larger, (supposedly) intellectually more important, and (certainly) environmentally more urgent issues have become the focus of design studios, research, and publication since at least the 1990s. Critical consideration of the physical making of the contemporary public realm? Not so much.

This reality quickly becomes evident in studio design reviews where discussions have principally become concerned with *issues* rather than physical interventions. Aspirations for environmental performance are privileged over spatial experience and material qualities. Processes—both natural and anthropogenic, ongoing and historic—have been elevated above tangible moments of spatial occupation. Abstract cartographic strategies have replaced measurable physical operations.

In this regard, it is not uncommon for design reviews to focus on "what a project

is about" or "concepts" rather than what is actually being proposed from the point of view of the constructed environment. As such, we are often left with illegible, abstract maps of "flows" and poorly crafted Photoshopped views that tell the viewer nothing beyond the fact that the author does not understand how perspectival space and vanishing points work. While this assessment may be a bit hyperbolic, the fundamental point remains: the public realm in American design pedagogy is treated as an afterthought – something seen as being simple and easy. Something seen to have limited intellectual value. Something that can—or worse, should—be learned in practice.

In thinking back to the question above—what's the project about?—I propose to use this essay to offer a simple provocation: what if the making of the public realm *was* the project? Both intellectually and physically, in policy and in material form, pedagogically and in practice. What if critical consideration of and engagement with the making of contemporary public space was the fundamental basis of a particular kind of design education and practice?

The Status of the Public Realm in the United States

Whereas the public realm in many societies is seen as an essential part of urban life, held up alongside housing, transport, and education as an essential component of urban society, such valuation does not exist in any commensurate way in the American context. Rather, in the United States, high-quality public space is principally seen simply as an amenity; an asset that is nice to have, but far less important than so-called essential public services like vehicular roads or water or police or garbage collection or broadband – utilities deemed necessary to daily life. Seemingly, the only way Americans are willing to make major *public* investments in the public realms of their cities and towns is if it is a mitigation feature of some other project that is considered actually essential; for example, coastal defense or the reconfiguration of a transport-related infrastructure. Otherwise, the making of high-quality public space in the US must rely on non-public motivators such as uncommon community advocacy, institutional and corporate philanthropy, or private real estate development.

There are, of course, myriad reasons why this is the case, but perhaps we can distill it down for our purposes here to one central consideration: the role land plays in both the politics and economy of the American society. While privately held property has long been the currency of power and influence, the shared public facility—specifically, truly accessible public space or the commons—has never risen to the level of importance and role it maintains in other economically mature quasi-democratic societies throughout the world. That is, unless it is shown to create additional economic value for adjacent property through increases in rents, density, or both.

And while limited capital investment in public space is a consistent challenge, public funding for maintenance and operations of existing public space in the United States has proven even more difficult to sustain. So, when municipal budgets need to be slashed—as was the case early in the pandemic prior to the disbursement of Federal relief funds—the first thing mayors and city councils look to cleave off are parks and recreation resources. This mentality is based on a value system that says these public facilities are optional, rather than indispensable contributors to public health, education, and environmental services.

Such a response really shouldn't be a surprise. The increasing reliance over the past 15 years on so-called pop-up public spaces, temporary activations, and placemaking interventions—particularly when these activities are not tied to any goal of longer-term, permanent transformation—is emblematic of the value system associated with public space in the United States. Rather than using political capital (and real capital!) to make meaningful investments in the public realm of a community that would have sustained, measurable societal benefits related to health, education, and the environment, disposable public spaces—so-called *activations*—have become the default. As a society, Americans both abstractly and in real terms under-value the public realm of their cities.

A Lack of Advocacy

In the context of the discussion above, it is perhaps interesting to consider that in the United States there is no real disciplinary advocate for the public realm. Or at least not one actively working to advance the role of public space in contemporary American society.[2] Other essential urban systems have recognized supporters across a range of disciplines that are engaged in policy, practice, research, and innovation related to the advancement of these systems (housing, transport, and education, for example). So why not the public realm? Where is the advocacy? Where are the data? Where is the interest in measuring and evaluating qualities? Where is the innovation, the experimentation?

As noted above, Americans simply do not prioritize the design of, investment in, or sustained maintenance of a high-quality public realm. And why would they when the discipline most often associated with its making—landscape architecture—doesn't seem to value the craft of making public space either? At least not in terms that can be seen within schools of design and the expressed concerns of affiliated professional organizations.

Consider for a moment the following: Over the last 25 years, the scale of landscape architecture's intellectual concerns has grown and grown and grown – from engagement with local landscapes, to regional ecologies, to, most recently, planetary concerns. And despite an engagement with the city and the urban implied by certain early-21st-century polemics, landscape architecture as a discipline has conspicuously avoided the middle, civic scale of public space crafting as a topic of critical engagement, in essence abdicating the professional responsibility for the shaping of these spaces.

The result is a discipline operating at two extremes, with the technical-oriented schools of design and smaller local practices choosing instead to remain content with decorative practices or elaborating community gardens, bioswales, and suburban subdivisions, while the institutions and practices considered to be at the leading intellectual edge of the discipline attempt to insert themselves into larger societal conversation around climate change mitigation strategies and racial inequity. Forgotten, both from the intellectual and practice perspective, is meaningful engagement with and sustained discourse around the actual making of public space in the contemporary city. A prioritization that renders examples of transformational public space projects in the United States as the exception, rather than the rule.

In this context, I would argue that the discipline of landscape architecture in the United States is missing an opportunity to claim the mantle of thought leadership and advocacy for the shaping of the urban public realm, instead allowing non-physical planners, civil engineers, and real estate developers to principally define what quality and caliber of public space is on offer in the contemporary American city. Taking up this opportunity would imply a focus on both the social and the physical; the form and the performance of urban spaces. Identifying and promoting not just the environmental services, but the transformative social potential of these spaces. It may seem obvious to the reader of this publication, but perhaps that familiarity is why it bears repeating. The public spaces of our cities have enormous power embedded within them—social, environmental, and infrastructural—but, at present, these potentially transformative powers remain untapped.

The Public Realm as Critical Enterprise

As is well known, the planet is confronted with monumental existential challenges – climate change, economic inequity, structural racism, violent nationalism, accelerating biodiversity loss, and increasing resource scarcity to name but a few. And always the happy warriors, the discipline of landscape architecture has selflessly turned its attention to many if not all these concerns, with the work of the discipline often framed as intentionally offering direct responses to these systemic urgencies. However well-intentioned, this preoccupation with the big issues often comes at the expense of local, physical design. That is, there is a growing dismissal—derision even—of the physical spatio-experiential consequences of a project as being secondary to the engagement with a larger systemic concern. The big idea or conceptual agenda is positioned—and more often than not, evaluated—as more critical than the actual physical intervention and resultant lived experiences.

Perhaps this treatment of the built reality and lived experience of a project as a secondary concern is a response to the inevitable negotiated realities to which actual physical design is subjected vis-à-vis cost, construction, client, and community concerns. Certainly, such an evaluation regularly occurs within the academy where there is limited exposure to what it takes to actually get things built in the United States, let alone things built of any real quality. These assessments often dismiss built outcomes as invariably corrupted and in turn deficient, unworthy of scholarly consideration while privileging ideas and ambitions that remain at the scale of rhetorical provocations or policy recommendations as somehow more powerful and worthy of discussion.

In Advocacy of Physical Design

What I believe this suggests is that physical design as both an intellectual concern and a professional activity must be elevated and made more accessible both within the academy and the public imagination. We must reject the conspiratorial notion that design is solely an instrument of capital, and instead understand it as a powerful tool open to potential appropriation. How and for what purpose this tool is ultimately used is up to those of us in the profession and in the academy, and to those who, in the future, we can bring into engagement with this work. Rather than dismissing physical design as unimportant, the academy has an obligation to elevate it. Through its teaching, its scholarship, and its own engagement with the construction of the built environment.

We are at a moment where students are increasingly coming into the discipline of landscape architecture wanting to be scientists or community organizers or activists. This is great: we should encourage these ambitions, but not at the expense of training the next generation of physical designers. Not at the expense of abdicating the shaping of public spaces that are, on the one hand, equitable, inviting, and sustainable, and on the other captivating, transformative, and essential. Physical design matters. Treating it as if it is something that is inevitable or unimportant or background is a disservice to the profession, to our cities and towns, to society, and the environment at large.

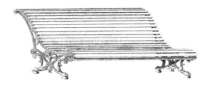

To achieve this repositioning within the academy, practice, and the public imagination, I believe that the public realm of contemporary human settlement must be understood and engaged by the discipline of landscape architecture simultaneously through three essential lenses: *the public realm as critical intellectual project; the public realm as essential urban infrastructure; and the public realm as focus of a renewed and urgently needed form of physical design praxis.* Pursuing this reframing will elevate the public consciousness of these most important spaces of our cities and towns, in turn connecting the populations who experience and occupy these spaces to the larger matrix of existential concerns with which these spaces are fundamentally intertwined.

With this in mind, I would like to conclude with what might be seen as a somewhat contrarian if not entirely quaint argument. That is, in lieu of engaging the wicked social and environmental problems mentioned above directly through the production of an abstract datascape or visually provocative cartography—big, non-spatial ideas—the critical landscape architectural practice might operate from the opposite direction. Working from the sensorial physical experiences of the individual body and the corresponding accumulation of collective public experiences as a means of reframing broader societal relationships to, and understanding of, these hyperobject-scaled concerns. Specifically, I am arguing for the value of engaging these existential challenges directly through the lens of constructing and reconstructing the American urban public realm. That is, engaging planetary and societal concerns through the making of human-scaled public space via physical design. Designing spaces to promote interplay and interaction between human and nonhuman worlds.

Such a position is rooted in the notion that if we want to create true stewards for the environment and a broader sense of social cohesion, landscape architecture should pay closer attention to the making of spaces where people interact and share common experience. That is, to have meaningful impact, the discipline must renew its focus on and consideration of the civic and quotidian spaces of urban public life. For it is in these public spaces where humanity and the environment's impossibly intertwined reality becomes most evident.

1. A note to the reader that I use the terms "public realm" and "public space" interchangeably throughout this essay to inclusively refer to all forms of publicly accessible physical space present within contemporary human settlement.

2. The excellent work of the Knight Foundation's Reimagining the Civic Commons program would be an exception to this point, though the focus there is principally on policy and capacity building.

INFORMALITY

David Gouverneur

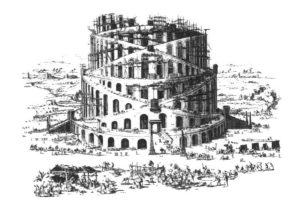

David Gouverneur is an associate professor of practice in landscape architecture and planning at the University of Pennsylvania's Weitzman School of Design. He is the author of *Planning and Design for Future Informal Settlements: Shaping the Self-constructed City* (2018), and is a professor emeritus of Universidad Rafael Urdaneta in Maracaibo, Venezuela.

I n the majority of developing countries, self-constructed peri-urban settlements are the dominant form of urbanization. Long considered slums and occluded from formal city planning instruments, informal urbanism does in fact have many virtues. The settlements tend to be very compact and pedestrian-friendly, their levels of energy consumption and waste are low, their fractal forms adapt to the topography, and strong community ties create a sense of place. Informal urbanism also offers residents the flexibility to expand and improve their homes, including income-generating activities such as small shops, rentals, and the possibility of selling parts of expanded homes. Over time, as it has throughout history, what begin as small and precarious settlements consolidate and expand into neighborhoods, districts, and eventually become large peri-urban cities.

It is ironic that many of the urban qualities that the contemporary formal city strives to achieve (walkability, density, and community) are commonplace in informal settlements, but we need to also be realistic about life in peri-urban self-constructed settlements. Life in informal settlements is tough: they typically lack infrastructure and public spaces, while basic services and violence come in waves. Better-paid jobs, services, and amenities are located in the formal city, forcing residents to commute long distances. They are frequently located on dangerous sites—floodplains, very steep terrain, brownfields, or under power lines—exposing communities to risks and health hazards. Informal urbanization also rapidly erodes agricultural land, pollutes waterways, and destroys remnant habitat, often in biodiverse regions.

World organizations, like the United Nations, predict that in only 25 years the population living in self-constructed settlements is expected to double, from the current one billion to two billion. While a percentage of this increment may occur by the gradual densification of existing settlements in self-constructed structures averaging three to five stories high, it is estimated that one-third of the new settlements will occupy peripheral land, eroding agricultural land, and natural habitats. My concern is that informal development is still considered taboo, illegal, and counterproductive in many of the cities where it is most commonplace. Pretending informal urbanization doesn't exist results in dangerous development and increased social tensions. Although governments and institutions acknowledge that informal urbanization will continue to grow exponentially, there is a lack of political will and technical vision to deal with informal urbanization preemptively. Beginning in academia at Universidad Simón Bolívar and later as National Director of Urban Development of Venezuela it has been my contention for over 30 years that we can maintain and enhance the positives of informal urbanism and eliminate the negatives through a design approach that is specifically tuned to the landscape conditions where it takes place.

As contradictory as this may seem, urban informality can and must be planned. What I refer to and explain below as the Informal Armatures Approach (IAA) is a method to engage with informal urbanism that I have developed through my studios at the Weitzman School of Design informed by my academic, professional, and public sector experience dealing with informality in Latin America. IAA is a hybrid method that not only accepts, but proactively anticipates informal growth and steers it away from high-level risk while at the same time underpinning it with a level of infrastructure, public space, communal facilities, productive activities, ecological services, and management that informal settlements would not otherwise achieve on their own. It is a new urban design method that carefully combines the planned and the unplanned and its structure is derived from understanding and appreciating the socio-economic conditions and landscape conditions in which informality takes root.

The IAA sets out a hybrid toolkit of simple design components: corridors, patches, and stewards. These components are not dogmatic in their nature, scale, or their morphological and performative qualities but they must be there in some form and interconnected with one another to form a matrix or landscape structure around which informality can accrue. The successful deployment of the corridors, patches, and stewards will depend on how local contextual and cultural nuances are taken into account, and on the ability of embedded IAA facilitators to engage with the communities and other urban actors.

There are two types of corridors: protector corridors and attractor corridors. The protector corridors are essentially multi-functional, linear landscapes kept free of urbanization (although urbanization is encouraged along their flanks). Oftentimes the protector corridors are related to remnant habitat, hydrology, and other ecological flows that should be connected and safeguarded while also including public recreational spaces and utilitarian uses such as small-scale food production and storm water retention. It is important to note, however, that in developing countries and particularly in predominantly informal areas, simply designating an area of land as non-urban doesn't make it so. The IAA method of protecting such landscape corridors is not to set them aside as "nature" or "park" but to fill them with multiple communal uses as quickly as possible so that by their very publicness they self-police against encroachment and privatization. The stewards, as explained below, also play a role here. Contrarily, attractor corridors serve to explicitly attract urban occupation, facilitating accessibility and mobility, concentrating infrastructure, utility lines, and services that require a certain economy of scale. These corridors are expected to densify and consolidate faster than other areas; they will become the more active and mixed-use corridors and include important civic spaces and edifices. The concentration of urban energy along the attractor corridors can also relieve urbanization pressure from the protector corridors.

The patches are tracts of land provided for urban infill, whether self-constructed, formal, or hybrid, predominantly residential, or to incorporate a diversity of uses of a local, urban, or metropolitan scale that rarely appear spontaneously within informal areas. The patches are defined and supported by the corridors. The patches have been divided into two categories: receptors and transformers. Receptor patches are tracts of land made available to the new settlers to begin erecting their dwellings, hence they are probably the component that the communities will most appreciate during the early phases of occupation. They offer the community an immediate sense of security, belonging, and hope for a better future, building their dwellings on lots that are in risk-free sites, legally assigned, embedded in neighborhoods and larger urban systems that will benefit from basic infrastructure, a system of open spaces, communal services, a diversity of uses, and public or institutional support. The lot sizes, provision of construction materials or an initial housing shell, the reservation of parcels to gradually incorporate neighborhood services, as well as the degree of assistance to help configure and foster the evolution of the receptor patches will be different in each context. Transformer patches are areas set aside that begin as one thing—say, a recycling center—but later, as the community evolves, become residential. The trick here again is to secure the spatial requirement related to necessary services that are relevant to the communities in different phases of evolution of the settlement. The transformer patches should be of a scale and at locations that in the future may be accessible and be able to serve larger populations and other programs as the settlement evolves. For example, over time patches can acquire small parks, technical schools, universities, hospitals, markets, and transportation centers. Transformer patches may also be used to gradually attract private investments in residential, mixed-use, office, or commercial projects.

Finally, the stewards are particular institutions that serve a community and by association—both real and perceived—safeguard the public realm around them. The stewards are preferably organizations, respected institutions, or service providers – things like schools, libraries, medical centers, churches, NGOs, sports centers, and food providers. Stewards offer passive surveillance of public space, prevent unwanted occupations, and can restrain development from environmentally sensitive and agriculturally productive areas. The stewards also anchor a community and build a sense of place.

During my academic and professional life, I have seen changing attitudes toward the informal city in my homeland Venezuela and other Latin American countries. The first informal settlements appeared in the periphery of Latin American cities toward the mid-20th century, as migrants fled rural economic hardships or violence and arrived in the cities seeking employment and services. In some cases, low-income families were displaced from inner-city neighborhoods to peripheral locations. In these early phases, the establishment naïvely believed that informality could be contained, eradicated by force, or relocated by providing public housing solutions. But the supply of housing always fell behind the demand, plus, in many cases, the dwellers could not afford the mortgages or pay the utilities, and so moved back to the informal settlements. Additionally, the self-constructed dwellings offered flexibility and a shadow economy, all of which was not possible in the social housing projects.

When the informal avalanche could not be halted, new occupations were tolerated in sites adjacent to the existing settlements and in other high-risk locations away from trendy areas, accentuating the already severe social and spatial fragmentation, the inequalities, and the cultural barriers of the Latin American societies that had been cemented during the colonial period. Socially discriminatory and technical arguments were used to justify why it was futile to formally recognize these areas: that to consolidate them was to consolidate misery and violence, and that because of their locations on high-risk terrain, investments to improve them would be wasted.

However, as informality became the dominant form of urbanization at the urban periphery, and most Latin American nations embraced democratic systems, new attitudes toward the informal city have emerged. Politicians realized that they had to capture votes, and thus local governments and political parties began providing basic communal services like water supply, electricity, paved access roads, pedestrian paths, public stairs, small sports facilities, and schools, as well as granting land titles, providing construction materials, and even organizing new squatting operations. The case studies that stand out as breakthroughs toward a more holistic approach to the informal city are those that were carried out in Medellín, Colombia, in the 1990s – a city that was considered the most dangerous in the world and is now a beacon of hope.

In the grip of Pablo Escobar's drug cartel in the 1980s and early 1990s, Medellín was infamous as the murder capital of the world. Remarkably, in 2013—just 20 years after Escobar was gunned down by American-funded paramilitaries—Medellín was hailed as the most innovative city in the world by the Urban Land Institute. How this transformation happened is due to a combination of good leadership and good urban design that accepted rather than denied the informal city. The catalyst for this was Mayor Sergio Fajardo's (2004–2008) concept of "social urbanism." Instead of razing the informal settlements and replacing them with government-issue housing, Fajardo—along with academics, community workers, and design professionals—not only accepted the reality of the informal city, but praised its strong sense of community, its social and aesthetic vibrancy, and levels of sustainability that planners can only dream of achieving in more formally designed cities. What the informal city needed, they realized, was not erasure and reconstruction, but acupunctural interventions to improve accessibility, connectivity, and basic services. Connected to innovative forms of public transport such as chairlifts and escalators to negotiate steep topography, institutions such as schools, medical centers, and libraries, as well as small parks have consequently now been strategically inserted into Medellín's periphery with transformative impact.

Nearly half of Colombia's 50 million people live in informal settlements, as do around two billion people worldwide, with many more inevitably to come. Medellín is a beacon of hope that these typically overlooked and under-served zones can be made safe, communal, productive, and edifying. Indeed, for the bulk of urban history humans have constructed their own settlements without top-down planning. If anything, it is the planned city, not the unplanned city, that is the aberration.

DATA

Robert Gerard Pietrusko

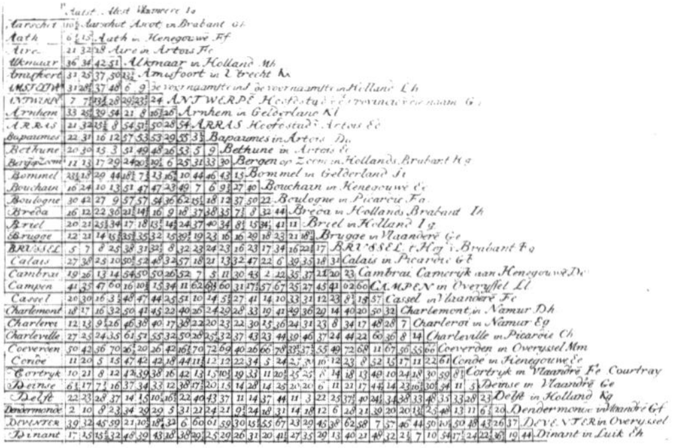

Robert Gerard Pietrusko is an associate professor of landscape architecture at the University of Pennsylvania Weitzman School of Design. His research and practice focus on the history and speculative design potential of environmental media. His design work is part of the permanent collection of the Fondation Cartier pour l'art contemporain in Paris and has been exhibited at the Museum of Modern Art in New York, the ZKM Center for Art & Media in Karlsruhe, and the Venice Architecture Biennale, among other venues.

I'd like to begin this essay with a brief and very specific history of the term "landscape." I offer a disclaimer that this will be reductive to the point of near caricature. My intention is not to clarify the messy and nuanced history of thinking about what landscapes are but to instead highlight one line of persistent thinking that relates to what I believe is a latent potential within the broader practice of landscape architecture – the direct engagement with environmental images and data, and their ability to change the broader social imagination.

Landscape, as is often repeated, was initially an art historical term. It emerged in the 17th century to describe a Western and Northern European painting style. Within this context, the concept of landscape specifically addressed the depiction of the natural world rather than denoting the natural world itself. It was the frame rather than the content that was of concern – framing and interpreting nature as landscape. Depiction in this sense was not merely recording what could be seen, instead landscapes constructed a view of the natural world with political underpinnings. They asserted a sovereignty over a territory and naturalized a set of spatial and social relationships, oftentimes directly in the service of state power. Even if one more accurately establishes the origin of landscape in ancient Rome or in the tradition of Chinese landscape paintings—as media theorist W.J.T. Mitchell[1] and many others have done—the practices of landscape in these examples remained tied to depiction rather than nature itself and asserted a dominion over that nature. In this way, they were closer to cartography in their operation than the fine arts. From these earliest conceptions, landscape implied a mediation of nature through images that showed the world not as it was but as the authors, or patrons, thought that it ought to be—spatially, socially, and politically—and it is this that places landscape firmly within the realm of design.[2]

The idea of a landscape never quite escaped its original conception: that whatever else it may be, landscape was also a form of representation – an image. During the 20th century, the concept of the cultural landscape assigned the seemingly *a priori* natural world, and patterns of human settlement within it, a representational function, and interpreted them as a "medium" of communication. Beginning with Carl Sauer in the 1920s and reaching its apex within Marxist geography in the 1980s, theorists understood the organization of a landscape as a surface appearance that expressed the underlying economic organization of society, most often capitalism.[3] The status of being a landscape was precisely this expression and to properly see it required deeper social and economic interpretation.

In the mid-20th century, images secured from an aerial perspective further exploited landscape's status as a communication medium. Cold War tensions between capitalist and communist countries made vast portions of the earth inaccessible for direct observation. With a desire to analyze all aspects of their adversaries' activities, intelligence officers secured aerial photographs of enemy landscapes and studied their patterns for evidence of military maneuvers, urban growth, crop health, and the location of natural resources. It wasn't the landscape itself that interested them but what the landscape indicated about a society that they could not observe directly. This way of reading the landscape later found civilian applications and was deployed by geographers and ecologists – many of whom had military affiliations.[4] Even today, as we look at satellite images of receding polar ice sheets or unexpectedly green fields in the Arctic, it is not the ice or the vegetation itself that we are seeing but rather an implicit visualization of human-induced climate change.

These thoughts about landscape images apply equally to spatial and environmental data. The distinction between imagery and data has long been difficult to maintain. The prevalence of remotely sensed imagery/data and use of raster formats in GIS have blurred this boundary since at least the 1970s and, more recently, data scientists have begun converting all manner of data into images to make them easier to process with contemporary machine-learning techniques. This apparently inconsequential technical detail has ontological implications. If the emergence of digital technology forced us to become comfortable with the idea that all imagery was in fact data, the opposite is now true: all data is actually imagery. In any case, environmental data and environmental images are more alike than different and their role as representation puts them both equally within the realm of landscape thinking.

But what does this all mean for landscape architecture? If, as geographer Denis Cosgrove writes, "landscape is a way of seeing," then it follows that in order to understand it we need to turn our attention to the modes through which landscape is represented as much as, if not more than, the thing itself.[5] It also follows that those who work with landscape visualization are well positioned to expand the popular imagination about our place within nature, both by interpreting the representations made and circulated by others, as well as creating such representations ourselves.

This is especially important now. With climate change, global pandemics, and an unstable and totalizing market economy, the factors that shape our experience of the world are primarily defined and understood through representations. These factors are so large and complex that it is difficult to place a boundary around them in any one place or at any one scale. Indeed, their defining qualities are conjured by our representations of them. As Fredric Jameson has said about capitalism, "no one has met or seen the thing itself," though we all have felt its effects.[6] We could easily say the same for the climate or any of the other hyperobjects that now comprise an increasingly unpredictable nature. If one of the tasks for landscape architecture is to construct an experience of nature for the public, it is this new nature that requires our framing and imagination. We should not merely interpret data or images but instead explore their potential meaning through a radical exegesis.[7] These themes have animated my design practice for the last decade, which has resulted in several "data documentary" installations that address the framing of the natural world through data. Beginning with important datasets that I wish to thematize and critique, I write custom software that performs data analysis and algorithmically generates dynamic visual narratives in response.

For example, *In Plain Sight* is a data documentary about global citizenship that challenges the most common interpretations of NASA's Black Marble – a popular image/dataset that depicts the earth through its nighttime illumination.[8] It is difficult to conceive of citizenship at this scale outside of our representations of the globe itself and it was precisely this property that we wanted to explore more fully, specifically by critiquing some of the most iconic depictions of the world to which different narratives of citizenship are attached. I believe that the piece highlights the relationship between landscape representations—in this case, at the scale of the whole earth—and the social imagination that they produce and support.

In December 1972, astronauts from the Apollo 17 mission took the first photograph that captured the whole earth within a single frame. This image—now known as the Blue Marble— connected with a contemporaneous discussion of global stewardship.[9] For many environmentalists in the 1970s, the earth was understood as a fragile "spaceship" that required ecologically minded care and maintenance. Like an earth-sized "mirror stage," the Blue Marble offered a unified image of a planet that, in one's everyday experience otherwise felt uncoordinated and fragmented.[10] Today the image remains iconic and continues to evoke an environmentalist discourse. Forty years later, NASA released a different view of the world: the Black Marble.[11] This image depicted the world illuminated at night, as measured by the orbiting Suomi satellite. Over the last two decades, these images have supported a neoliberal narrative of global citizenship, where one is a cosmopolitan agent traversing a borderless world without friction. This citizen is no longer a steward of the environment but is instead immersed in a global economy of ever-flowing capital and information shaped by patterns of intense urbanization – all running indifferent to international borders.[12]

It is important to note that aside from its role as an image, the Black Marble is also used as a dataset in support of this view of the world and is often referred to as "Night Lights" data. Geographers and urbanists use this dataset to delineate more precise boundaries for urban areas—beyond conventional municipal borders—or more provocatively, to provide evidence for new urban categories. For instance, urban megaregions such as "BosWash" in the US or the "Blue Banana" in Europe appear as constellations in the Night Lights even as they lack a unified existence that can be registered through means other than satellite imagery.

The Blue and Black Marbles are not only related in name but also in how they are created. Though quite different from the original 1972 photograph, NASA still publishes images of the visible earth during different seasons under the name Blue Marble.[13] Like the Black Marble, these images are collected by the Suomi satellite, which descends the front face of the earth in the daytime, producing the Blue Marble, and ascends the back face of the earth in darkness, producing the Black Marble. It is a subtle but profound point: one satellite producing two images that imply definitions of global citizenship in contradiction with each other, both environmentally and politically.[14]

Both the Blue and Black Marble are representations in service of conventional tropes about globalism and global citizenship. Like the Blue Marble, the Black Marble presents the world as matter-of-fact. Whether one is for or against global forms of urbanism, there seems to be no question about what is being depicted in the image's pixels – a borderless and expansive development, indicated by illumination. The Black Marble appears to naturalize this condition. In so doing, it seems to foreclose other understandings of what is being depicted as well as other information communicated by the landscape. But if landscape is, as Cosgrove says, "a way of seeing," then what is required to "see" this landscape, to interpret its patterns differently? *In Plain Sight* challenges the story of a frictionless globalism that is seemingly depicted in the pixels of the Night Lights dataset. Counter to the idea that the world is now borderless, *In Plain Sight* demonstrates that nation states and numerous types of boundaries are still a persistent feature of people's experience of globalism. The Night Lights might appear as a smooth surface of continuous settlement but its brightness actually indicates a politics of electrification and the uneven distribution of resources.

Instead of focusing on the Night Lights' bright pixels, *In Plain Sight* also looks closely at pixels in the dark. To do this we created a taxonomy of 16 alternative definitions of citizenship, each describing a specific condition of brightness or darkness within the Black Marble image and combined Night Lights with another very common global dataset, the Gridded Population of the World (GPW), published by the Center for International Earth Science Information Network.[15] The demographers who create this dataset have the ambition of counting every person on earth and each pixel in GPW attempts to establish how many people are living in the associated location. Our categories emerged from exploring the gaps between these two datasets and highlighted conditions that fell outside of how both represented citizenry. We created the gaps through a simple subtractive operation familiar to any landscape architect – we merely looked at areas where the datasets did not correspond spatially. This resulted in two primary conditions: locations where there were people (as indicated by GPW) but no light, and locations where there was light (as indicated by the Night Lights) but no people. These conditions allowed us to challenge the conventional narratives surrounding the Black Marble image.

Though the Black Marble is overwhelmingly composed of dark pixels, one tends to focus on the brightness. And yet, located in the dark pixels are many contemporary conditions that perhaps better describe the current state of global capitalism and its citizens than the well-lit urban corridors that are otherwise so charismatic. To look at the darkness, *In Plain Sight* visually sampled numerous dark pixels that had significant population counts and found other forms of settlement and related stories: refugee camps, informal urban settlements, locations suffering from power outages, settlements of people working for mineral extraction companies, wealthy enclaves that can influence city ordinances against light pollution, cities that are denied lights for political reasons, isolated villages, and indigenous territories. Despite showing up as dark spots, each of these settlements communicates the complexity of contemporary life under global capitalism and is clearly present when explored through other satellite images. Within these eight classes, *In Plain Sight* employed data-mining techniques to find hundreds of instances and visualized them both as a matrix and as a global pattern.

Inversely, we also identified locations where lights were present on the Black Marble but were unpopulated according to the GPW, a condition we called "Lights-No People." When inspected through other satellite imagery, these locations contained many highly urbanized forms that were not conventional settlements, and again we chose to highlight eight of them: international borders, industrial farms, power plants, ports, natural gas refineries, mines, military bases, and tourism destinations. To be clear, our designation of "Lights-No People" applied strictly to the demographic data, as it appeared in the GPW. Here, "no people" means that no people are officially recorded as living there. *In Plain Sight*, however, challenges the idea that people are categorically absent from these locations and argues instead that every bright but unpopulated place has a profound relationship to a population – living in the dark and potentially underserved. What one sees when looking at the lights is a concentration of resources that oftentimes sidesteps citizens within close proximity. *In Plain Sight* explored the relationship between sites with "Lights-No People" and adjacent populations through up-close narratives about four of the above categories. For the sake of length, I will only describe two of them in more detail.

The first example is the KOV open-pit copper mine located in the southeast corner of the Democratic Republic of Congo (DRC). It is operated by Glencore, an Anglo-Swiss conglomerate that owns extraction sites all over the globe. Given the scale of its operations, KOV has extensive power requirements that are supplied by the Inga Dam hydro-electric power plant located in the northwestern part of the DRC. Though the two locations are separated by several thousand kilometers, they are connected by a single high-voltage power line that cuts across the entire country.

Like the Inga Dam, the power line is a massive piece of infrastructure and as it traverses the country its path runs adjacent to numerous cities, towns, and villages that are unable to extract power from it. These settlements often experience frequent power outages, while the KOV mine is guaranteed constant power. The discrepancies in illumination are clearly seen in the Black Marble and communicate the uneven access to resources: the KOV mine and the Inga Dam are brightly lit, whereas settlements along the power line remain in the dark. On the one hand, the DRC government mobilizes a massive infrastructural project to support the operations of a multinational company, while on the other hand, the DRC's inhabitants receive unstable electricity. I use the word inhabitant instead of citizen because illumination raises the question of who is, indeed, a citizen in this case. If one of the primary functions of a contemporary nation state is to metabolize its natural resources for the benefit of its citizens, then it appears that a Swiss mining company has a stronger claim to citizenship than many people who live in the DRC. Similar questions emerge when looking at the next site, the Punta Cana tourist resort in the Dominican Republic.

Along the north and east coast of the Dominican Republic, one can see a pattern of bright illumination on the Black Marble. Likewise, numerous buildings are clearly visible when consulting satellite imagery. However, the official population in these locations is zero. This region is the Punta Cana resort area – a vast enclave supported by an exclusive power grid that is completely separate from the rest of the island. The inhabitants of the Dominican Republic are otherwise served by a public power supply that is unreliable and prone to outages, as demonstrated by the Black Marble in which these small towns are depicted as entirely dark. The separation between these two populations is not complete as most of the resort's employees reside in these inland towns; their labor supports the operation of the resorts, but they do not benefit from the superior infrastructure. The GPW depiction of zero population is therefore even more ironic. Like the case of the KOV mine, Punta Cana highlights a situation where a nation state has the technology and the will to create resources for those who reside there, however, these residents are tourists, not Dominican citizens. *In Plain Sight* used techniques of data-mining to locate hundreds of similar sites around the globe.

So far it may seem that my argument is that some nation states treat global companies and global travelers more like citizens than their own people. While this is indeed the case, I also believe that these case studies highlight a more compelling definition of a "global citizen" that is the opposite of this apparent argument. Much like the Black Marble itself, a truer depiction is found with a figure-ground inversion, focusing on the black pixels more than on the bright ones. The overriding experience of being a global citizen for many people on earth is to exist in a precarious condition adjacent to the forces of global capitalism. They witness firsthand its incredible powers of mobilization. Their labor is likely enlisted in its reproduction, and yet they are not able to directly reap its benefits. Is this not what is actually depicted in the Black Marble?

As we have seen, landscape representations often naturalize what they depict. As images circulate, their mute matter-of-factness seems to claim that they only show things as they are, and—by their implied naturalism— how things ought to be. But interpreting images in this way also naturalizes the spatial, ecological, and political relations that produced them, as well as the dominant narratives used to describe them. This is the subtle, diffuse, and conservative power of environmental images. Counter to this tendency, however, the notion of "ought to be" also has a powerful public function that is central to the concept of the Social Imaginary developed by philosopher, Charles Taylor.[16] The Imaginary is a collective mental model held by a particular society. It shapes the individual's imagination as to how they fit into the world and what their potentials are; it establishes expectations for how things unfold naturally and as a result for how things ought to unfold. As political scientist Chiara Bottici elaborates, the social imaginary is deeply entangled with images that reinforce a particular perceived horizon of possibility.[17] It is through alternative narratives of current images, and the creation of entirely new ones that changes in the social imaginary are enacted and radical collective actions become possible. With a new imagination, new expectations for how the world ought to unfold circulate and take root.

If landscape has long been a medium that frames our relationship to the natural world and depicts the socio-economic forces that shape it, what might be the political efficacy of a landscape imaginary? As *In Plain Sight* demonstrates, even images that appear matter-of-fact can contain a multitude of descriptions of how things are but certainly not as they ought to be. Within this new imaginary, landscape architects might conceive of themselves in a new role: critiquing common environmental images and data; deriving new, more productive categories for describing them; and proposing entirely new representations in their place. It may be through landscape as a medium that we expand the possibility for imagining a radically new relationship to the natural world.

1. W.J.T. Mitchell, "Imperial Landscape," in W.J.T. Mitchell (ed.), *Landscape and Power*, 2nd ed. (University of Chicago Press, 2002), 1–34.

2. Herbert A. Simon, The Sciences of the Artificial, 3rd ed. (The MIT Press, 1996), 111; c.f. D.J. Huppatz, "Revisiting Herbert Simon's 'Science of Design,'" *Design Issues* 31, no. 2 (2015): 29–40.

3. Carl Sauer, *The Morphology of Landscape* (Berkeley University Press, 1925), 300–11; James Duncan & Nancy Duncan, "(Re) reading the Landscape" *Environment and Planning D: Society and Space* 16 (1988): 117–26; Denis Cosgrove, "Towards a Radical Cultural Geography: Problems of Theory" *Antipode* 15, no. 1 (1983): 1–11.

4. Robert Pietrusko, "Ground Cover," *LA+ Journal of Landscape Architecture* 12 (2020).

5. Denis Cosgrove, *Social Formation and the Symbolic Landscape* (University of Wisconsin Press, 1984), xiv.

6. Fredric Jameson, "Cognitive Mapping" in Cary Nelson & Lawrence Grossberg (eds), *Marxism and the Interpretation of Culture* (University of Illinois Press, 1988), 354.

7. Radical in two senses: in the thoroughness of our image-reading, and in the potential for alternative political outcomes.

8. *In Plain Sight* was coproduced with Elizabeth Diller and Laura Kurgan for the 2018 Venice Architecture Biennale where the curatorial theme for the US pavilion was "Dimensions of Citizenship." Seven design teams were invited to explore the concept of citizenship at seven increasing scales. We were assigned the scale of the whole earth.

9. NASA, "Visible Earth: The Blue Marble from Apollo 17." Data acquired December 7, 1972, https://visibleearth.nasa.gov/images/55418the-blue-marble-from-apollo-17.

10. Jacques Lacan on the mirror stage: "the subject originally identifies himself with the visual Gestalt of his own body: in relation to the still very profound lack of co-ordination of his own motility, it represents an ideal unity, a salutary imago": Jacques Lacan, *Ecrits*, trans. Bruce Fink (W.W. Norton & Co, 2006), 18–19.

11. NASA, "NASA's Black Marble," https://blackmarble.gsfc.nasa.gov/.

12. Parag Khanna, *Connectography: Mapping the Future of Global Civilization* (Random House, 2016), 3–57.

13. NASA, "The Next Generation Blue Marble," https://www.nasa.gov/vision/earth/features/blue_marble.html.

14. This irony is amplified if we assume that the economic and urban patterns registered in the Black Marble are the same forces that make the earth ecologically fragile, and therefore require the iconic Blue Marble to mobilize an environmental awareness.

15. Center for International Earth Science Information Network, "Gridded Population of the World, Version 4 (GPWv4): Population Count," (NASA Socioeconomic Data and Applications Center), http://dx.doi.org/10.7927/H4X63JVC.

16. Charles Taylor, *Modern Social Imaginaries* (Duke University Press, 2004).

17. Chiara Bottici, *Imaginal Politics: Images Beyond Imagination and the Imaginary* (Columbia University Press, 2014).

MODELING

Karen M'Closkey & Keith VanDerSys

Karen M'Closkey & Keith VanDerSys are directors of PEG office of landscape + architecture and cofounders of the Environmental Modeling Lab at the University of Pennsylvania Weitzman School of Design. Their work focuses on the opportunities and limitations enabled by advancements in digital modeling, and how the assumptions embedded in our methods and tools shape our understanding of landscapes and environments. Their work has been acknowledged through numerous publications, awards, exhibitions, and fellowships, including a PEW Fellowship in the Arts. They are authors of *Dynamic Patterns: Visualizing Landscapes in a Digital Age* (2017), and guest editors of *LA+ SIMULATION* (2016) and *LA+ GEO* (2020).

I t has been just over two decades since landscape architect James Corner wrote his influential essay "The Agency of Mapping: Speculation, Critique and Invention," which came only 10 years after J.B. Harley's now canonical "Deconstructing the Map." In it, Corner quotes Harley that "Maps are too important to be left to cartographers alone."[1] Like the human and cultural geographers who were alarmed at the increasingly quantitatively driven nature of their broader field, Corner's critique was directed toward the limitations of analytical surveys of existing conditions – or "tracings."[2] Through outlining various mapping techniques, his essay was aimed at designers, prodding them to expand their tools and methods and, he hoped, their imaginations. It emphasized process over product, mapping over map. The flurry of literature in the 1980s and 1990s that critiqued analytical or "normative" mapping methods is taken for granted today. It is widely acknowledged that maps are highly selective and politically motivated representations and not simply depictions of "actual" conditions. It is also recognized that mapping practices were and are far more diverse and messier than what cartography proper would allow. And it has been demonstrated that GIS—the subject of derision by some critics—can be used to reinforce the status quo or directed to undermine it.[3] Meanwhile, the tools for mapping and access to extant maps and data continue to grow exponentially. Innumerable articles, journals, books, and drawings—from a wide array of disciplines and individuals—attest to the enduring centrality of mapping to understanding and depicting spatial and temporal relationships.

At the time of writing "The Agency of Mapping," Corner felt that mapping and other spatial design techniques had yet to creatively engage "the dynamic and promiscuous character of time and space," particularly "in a world where local economies and cultures are tightly bound into global ones."[4] He likened the map surface to a staging ground for collecting and sorting disparate materials, structured so as not to align in scale or position. This hybridity promotes a multifaceted reading of landscapes by incorporating many kinds of information and orientations of which the planimetric map is but one piece. With this approach, a mapmaker is thereby free to associate independent layers that represent a more extensive or varied understanding of context or place than what a uniformly scaled and hierarchically ordered map would allow.[5] Corner's critique of tracings is akin to Bruno Latour's claim that "one should not confuse projection with connectivity: the data are richer in connectivity than are the (inevitably limited) projections used to organize them."[6] By this characterization, projection and scale are freed from their cartographical definitions—orthographic projection and map scale—or at least not constrained by them. Such "non-cartographic" or "materialist" conceptions of scale were central to the expansion of maps beyond their normative definition—a two-dimensional, scaled representation of the earth's surface, or some part of it—to include a much broader array of images.[7]

This more encompassing understanding of mapping has, according to Jill Desimini and Charles Waldheim, "generated an unintended looseness to mapping in design culture."[8] In their book *Cartographic Grounds*, they argue that depictions that favor "the intangible over the material" have gained ascendency and cite Corner's "The Agency of Mapping" as having contributed to liberating the map from the ground.[9] Criticism of the rise of such approaches to mapping is not limited to landscape architecture. Concerns about the groundlessness of much data visualization, and the ubiquity of maps that illustrate networks and flows without regard to local conditions, have only increased in the last two decades. For example, in "Time for Mapping," Thomas Sutherland describes flow maps as marking a "turn away from the representation of space toward the spatialization of time."[10] While he does not discount the efficacy of flow maps, he says they support "a mythology of a frictionless capitalism" that "smooths over the disjunctures and dissymmetries that characterize the global economy."[11] Likewise, Heather Houser discusses the plethora of visualizations about environmentally detrimental activities whereby artists and designers make maps, graphs, flowcharts, and animations using data provided by others. This "InfoViz" is geared toward lay audiences and employs a "connect the dots" aesthetic to represent economic or environmental interconnectedness.[12] Houser argues that such lines of connection are the "dominant geometry of environmental discourse" and warns that the pressure to make environmental issues transparent and digestible overly simplifies the narrative that these visualizations are meant to convey. Other scholars similarly note that the combination of readily available digital technologies and the existential threat of global warming has "produced a new and urgent impulse to visualize in order to exert control" and that "synoptic map[ping] contributes to the formation of political inequalities" when such views are scaled down to local situations.[13]

In response to these trends in mapping, Desimini and Waldheim seek to re-instill a close attention to terrain in order to reunite the plan and the map.[14] They do so by focusing on representational techniques that describe the form and material of the earth's surface, namely topographic, bathymetric, and landcover maps, and by emphasizing "precision" and "projection" as a means toward this reengagement with ground. The dual meaning of projection is important; it necessitates understanding the translation of three-dimensional entities onto two-dimensional surfaces—geometric projection—and it also refers to planning for future possibilities. Though there has always been a close relationship between the two definitions—surveys are used to make maps, which are subsequently used to make plans and territory—never has the conceptual and representational gap between projection as survey of ground and projection as making plans seemed so large.

Our knowledge about the climate crisis has led to the proliferation of representations of global environmental trends rendered visible through scientific climate models and images like InfoViz described above, yet the uncertainty inherent in such projections has exacerbated the difficulty of linking global trends to the local places and people affected by rapid environmental change. One of the more prevalent and popular types of visualization intended to relate satellite-derived views and global change models to specific places are online tools such as NOAA's Sea Level Rise Viewer.[15] This slider tool enables zooming in both space and time – one can look up a location and see what happens at a regional or city level using varying parameters for sea level rise.[16] A number of authors have recently disparaged this so-called "Zoom" effect using a well-known video from the 1970s as the object of their scorn. They describe Charles and Ray Eames's "Powers of Ten" as a predecessor of Google Earth because it creates an illusion that masks the fact that the images used to produce the zoom effect of smoothness and continuity are obtained from radically different sources. Latour goes so far as to claim that "Powers of Ten" led artists and scientists astray: "good artists do *not* believe in zoom effects."[17] Others have made similar points by calling for the incorporation of non-cartographic concepts of scale that consist of "jumps and discontinuities," or "breaks, disjunctures and striations" that show the contingency of our representations.[18] Still others remind us of earlier calls for such approaches, for example Donna Haraway's "partial perspective" and John Pickle's "cartographic bricolage," characteristics that were central to Corner's framing and use of particular techniques in "The Agency of Mapping" and, earlier, *Taking Measures Across the American Landscape*.[19] The importance of such methods is that they lay bare the constructed nature of images in ways that the smoothness of InfoViz, the scalar zoom of Google Earth, or the orthographically aligned layers of GIS mapping elide. Artists, designers, scholars, and map makers of every stripe continue to demonstrate that place-based representations should not be confined to quantifiable and measurable considerations and thus maps should not be constrained by a Euclidean understanding of space where "interoperability" among datasets is presumed.[20]

While non-cartographic representations of scale—connections not projections—are required to promote a multifaceted understanding of context and environment, if one is to actually *make plans*, as landscape architects do, then the two kinds of projection (geometric and propositional) need to be brought into alignment. The problem of zooming, as argued by these various authors, is that it gives the appearance of continuity by collapsing disparate scales, resolutions, and sources. We agree, however, the problem should not be blamed on projections per se but when those projections are invisibly mismatched, as with the zoom-effect, or worse, unknowingly mismatched, which is our concern and the crux of our argument below. This is especially true for designers working on projects in coastal and low-lying inland areas under a warming climate and growing uncertainty about the rate of environmental change.

Datums: Projection, Precision, and Accuracy

When Corner states that the design and set-up of the mapping field—which includes units of measure, extents of frame, and projection system   is "one of the most creative acts in mapping [because it] condition[s] how and what observations are made," he was not limiting his approach to descriptions of topography and elevation, as we do below. In landscape architecture these factors are elemental. To be clear, such grounding will not be any more likely to *lead to* a plan than will the layered map-drawings described by Corner or the topographic maps featured in *Cartographic Grounds*. Any of these maps may or may not initiate design proposals. Rather, bringing the two meanings of projection into alignment is a critical starting point for the basis of any plan. In this regard, we agree with the argument put forth in *Cartographic Grounds* that there needs to be more attention to terrain and not just what "flows" across it; however, many of the examples in the book would not provide a bridge to making plans that "afford greater proximity to the manifestation and manipulation of the ground itself" because they do not contain the information needed to do so.[21] According to its authors, the purpose of *Cartographic Grounds* is to realign data, broadly understood, with "geographic fidelity."[22] But what about the data that is used to create that geographic fidelity in the first place?

As stated by Corner and others, the "map precedes the territory" and, according to Desimini and Waldheim, the "map precedes the plan," or at least they believe it should. Of course, the survey precedes the map and it is possible to proceed from survey directly to a plan or design proposition without intermediary maps. This process is made easier with the advent of the global positioning system (GPS), leading some to ask what purpose maps serve now that we have such technology.[23] Anyone with a smart phone can locate their position within a 7-to-20-meter horizontal accuracy, which is good enough for some purposes and potentially lethal for others. For landscape architects, that level of accuracy is fine for navigation but not particularly helpful when it comes to design. Rather than think of GPS as a virtual overlay on extant map layers such as topography and roads, it is important to recognize the substantial shift that has occurred since "The Agency of Mapping" was written given the widespread availability of geo-referenced data made possible through GPS. This does not so much "free" us from the map as it does lead to changes in how maps are made and used.

The Agency of Modeling

Surveying with remote sensing technologies and satellite positioning enables the creation of detailed topographic and bathymetric models, but this assumes one understands how this information is gathered and how to produce it oneself. Though GPS has revolutionized how locational data is derived, establishing common points of reference—horizontal and vertical datums—is not as straightforward as it may seem, especially when water is brought into play.

Though mapping the land-water interface may appear to be more "seamless" with GPS and remote sensing it is not without its complexities, not least because coastal morphology and water presence are ever changing but also because the datums themselves are changing. Datums are, simply, agreed upon points of reference, which vary by country, state, and institution, and yet they are the basis for guiding many coastal management policies and land use regulations, not to mention their use in models for studying storm surge and sea level rise. No measure is without some uncertainty and inaccuracy regardless of the method used to obtain such information; however, one should not compound this uncertainty with errors related to projection systems.

Different datums are based on different projection systems and these projections—both geometric and predictive—play a significant role in how all coastlines are drawn. According to Mark Monmonier, the latter part of the 20th century not only saw significant technological advancements in remote sensing and GIS but also the development of what he terms the third and fourth coastlines.[24] The first two lines—high and low water—have long been depicted on coastal charts and topographic maps, whereas the third and fourth depict the element of time in particular ways. These third and fourth coastlines are not based on a physical distinction between land and water, but rather a statistical one inferred from historical records and predictive models. As changeable and inexact as the first and second coastlines are, they are nevertheless based on physical observation, such as wrack lines and tide gauges. Third shorelines are imaginary and arbitrary designations based on rainfall and storm surge estimates, which are used to delineate flood plains for insurance and land use decisions. Fourth shorelines are sea level rise projections and thus have unknown timeframes due to the high degree of variability and uncertainty resulting from a rapidly warming planet. For a field that is involved in designing around or with these projections, landscape architects should understand and acknowledge the presumptions of our best laid plans.

Landscape architects are good at precision. It is a quality that is often discussed in terms of specificity and craft – an attention to detail, care about material assemblies, the line work of a drawing, and so on. Accuracy on the other hand (at least with respect to datums) is how that "precise" and well-crafted design is situated with respect to its physical context. Unless a specific agency or city has contracted localized surveying and modeling, much of the geospatial data and extant maps that a designer would obtain are derived from satellite and aerial remote sensing. Working on regional plans with broad prescriptions does not always require more accuracy than this; however, at the scale and size that projects are designed, approved, and constructed, this inaccuracy makes a world of difference. In this way, the distinction between precision and accuracy is important, particularly when determining topographic elevations.

Land elevations are based on one of two mathematical models that approximate the earth's shape: ellipsoids and geoids. There are many of each type, developed by different countries and institutions at different times; therefore, translating among datums is one the most prevalent and important geospatial tasks. The elevations derived using GPS—typically represented as digital elevation models (DEMs)—use an ellipsoid as their reference, whereas the contours shown on topographic maps such as those produced by the USGS are based on distance from a geoid.[25] Thus, GPS elevations and those of topographic maps exist with respect to different datums and must be translated mathematically to align. For example, the difference between the zero elevation of a geoid and that of an ellipsoid along the Louisiana coast would constitute roughly 27 meters.[26] In other words, if one were to derive elevations directly from a DEM, they would be wrong. Working in familiar areas or along coasts one would likely realize a mistake of this magnitude but, otherwise this error would only be found if comparing the DEM to an existing topographic map.

The difficulty of setting a datum is further complicated when it comes to mapping bathymetry (earth's surface under water). Topographers and hydrographers use different methods and datums for their respective surveys.[27] This leads to discrepancies in land-water elevations, and thus inconsistencies in property delineation, flood maps, wetland extent, and so on. Unlike land, neither human sight nor aerial-based sensing can easily see beneath the surface of the water.[28] Topography can be referenced geodetically, as described above, but mapping bathymetry requires sonar and a tidal datum. Tidal datums are themselves problematic since they are an average elevation calculated over 19 years. The shorelines depicted on USGS topographic maps do not match those of NOAA's nautical charts and, prior to 2001, it was not even possible to match them in a topobathy model, which remains true of any area without a vertical datum.[29] As mentioned above, translating among various datums is essential for anyone working with geospatial data; it is also one of the most complicated tasks to understand and one of the easiest to botch. One tragic example of this mistake was the levee overtopping in New Orleans during Hurricane Katrina. Most people know that the levees failed structurally – as surge overtopped them the force of water eroded the backsides causing their collapse. But many may not know that overtopping would have been reduced if not for a datum mix up. Sections of the levee were built two feet lower than their designed elevations because of an "inaccurate relationship" between the geodetic datum and mean sea level (MSL).[30] Along the coast, the geoid and MSL are assumed to be the same, but that is only true if the correct geoid datum is chosen.

The potential for mismatched datums will only increase as datums are added and updated and the rate of coastal change from subsidence and erosion increases. Knowing how data line up in time is as important as their spatial projection. Furthermore, the fourth shoreline of sea level rise is shifting all the others at a rate that cannot be predicted with any degree of accuracy. So why bother working with these datums at all? We would argue that the agency of landscape architects in this context is to visualize the specificity of conditions on the ground including the inaccuracies and uncertainties of our representations, and that requires understanding the information upon which they are based. While landscape architects may choose the cartographic scale of a particular map, the information contained within it has likely been gathered at different resolutions and times by different agencies with different agendas. Resolution precedes questions of map scale. In fact, the two are unrelated. A recent study showed that there are 40 million people in the USA living within the 100-year floodplain—part of the "third shoreline"—compared to the previous estimate of 13 million, a finding based simply on using finer resolution data.[31] In one regard, this number is meaningless because we cannot design our way out of a floodplain at a continental scale; however, it is an indication of the relationship among models, maps, and physical ground. Floodplain designations determine what is allowed to get built, and where, and lower resolution information directly impacts how these lines get drawn. The same scale of map can show widely divergent coastlines.

The flip side of this example is what is excluded from this imaginary third coast since it is based on a threshold of "event" that does not account for so-called minor flooding. These minor events, which greatly impact people's lives, escape the resolution of flood modeling and mapping and often occur outside of designated flood zones.[32] In other words, information represented in extant map sources is limited to that which can be captured with current sensing technologies and surveying practices, and those are the standards by which much landscape practice is delimited. To understand topography with respect to its context requires augmenting extant maps and models with near-ground or on-ground surveying, which for client-driven work is provided by a surveyor hired to do the job. However, landscape practice is not restricted to such work, nor should it be given that too many projects are delimited by a timeframe that is insufficient for the physical and conceptual transformation that is needed.

Our knowledge of the causes and pace of climate change is made possible by global change science, but the ways in which we design for this change is not about scaling up to bigger and bigger projects. Problems considered global in scale cannot be addressed at that scale and, when they are, they often contribute to inequities. Nor can we simply zoom in on extant maps and models. Perhaps the larger point is that the synoptic view is not a question of map scale or distance from the ground but rather an attitude toward mapping. In other words, one does not have to be high in the sky to employ a synoptic or globalized view. Much of the waterfront development that continues apace in cities around the world—comprised of precisely detailed and well-crafted designs—employs such a view. At the same time, just because one uses, or makes, data and inventories does not mean one makes tracings. Critical practices can arise out of critical cartography, neo-geography, and many other approaches to mapping, but it also can arise from within conventional mapping techniques if the purpose is to examine how those conventions are derived and employed. If there is anything that the 1980s and 1990s perspectives on mapping taught us, it is that we should not delimit what a map is or should be. In practice, there is only mapping.[33] "Undisciplined" mapping is an ongoing and always relevant endeavor, but so is the question of what falls within the purview of landscape architecture and what constitutes its craft. There are many answers to this question. The landscape project is broad, and design by any means is an act of imagination. However, when it comes to making topographic models and maps as intermediaries to direct this imagination toward a future that will not resemble the lines on our current maps, connections and projections must go hand in hand.

1. James Corner, "The Agency of Mapping: Speculation, Critique and Invention," in Denis Cosgrove (ed.), *Mappings* (Reaktion Books, 1999), 221; J.B. Harley, "Deconstructing the Map," *Cartographica* 26, no. 2 (1989). Corner's quote references an abstract in a later version of Harley's essay. See Trevor J. Barnes & James S. Duncan (eds), *Writing Worlds* (Routledge, 1992), 231.

2. Corner, "The Agency of Mapping," 213–14. Corner borrows from Deleuze and Guatarri who argue that maps are projective whereas "tracings" reproduce what is presumed to be known and involve "alleged competence."

3. Indeed Matthew H. Edney contends that cartography must die because it is an ideal that has no bearing in practice and yet forms the basis around which all critiques of mapping are based. See Edney, *Cartography: the Ideal and Its History* (University of Chicago Press, 2019).

4. Corner, "The Agency of Mapping," 226.

5. On the use of collage and montage in landscape architecture in the 1980s and 1990s, see Karen M'Closkey, "Structuring Relations: From Montage to Model in Composite Imaging," in Charles Waldheim & Andrea Hansen, (eds), *Composite Landscapes: Photomontage and Landscape Architecture* (Hatje Cantz and Isabella Stewart Gardner Museum, 2015), 116–31.

6. Bruno Latour, "Anti-zoom," http://www.bruno-latour.fr/node/608.

7. The phrase "non-cartographic concepts of scale" is from Timothy Clark, "Scale," in Tom Cohe (ed.), *Telemorphosis: Theory in the Era of Climate Change*, Vol 1 (Open Humanities Press, 2014); and "materialist conception of scale" is from Chris Tong, "Ecology without Scale: Unthinking the World Zoom," *Animation: An Interdisciplinary Journal* 9, no. 2 (2014): 198. Tong states that "scale is a product of social construction rather than an epistemological grid mapped onto absolute space," 198–99. As numerous scholars have written, these aspects have always been part of mapping, just not part of a narrowly defined cartography.

8. Jill Desimini & Charles Waldheim, *Cartographic Grounds: Projecting the Landscape*

Imaginary (Princeton Architectural Press, 2016), 17.

9. Ibid., 9.

10. Thomas Sutherland, "Mapping the Space of Flows: Considerations and Consequences," in Sybille Lammes et. al (eds), *Time for Mapping: Cartographic Temporalities* (Manchester University Press, 2018), 176.

11. Ibid., 192–93.

12. Heather Houser, "The Aesthetics of Environmental Visualizations: More than Information Ecstasy?" *Public Culture* 26, no. 2 (2014): 321.

13. Douglas Robb & Karen Bakker, "Planetary Voyeurism," *LA+ Interdisciplinary Journal of Landscape Architecture* 12 (2020) 50. Also see Birgit Schneider & Lynda Walsh, "The Politics of Zoom: Problems with Downscaling Climate Visualizations," *GEO: Geography and Environment* (2019). The authors describe a reforestation effort that was deemed successful by scientists and international agencies but not so by farmers because the scientists, using satellite images, counted shrubs as trees whereas the farmers did not. Similar arguments can be found in Alan M. Berger & Johan Susskind, "The Planetary Optic and Finding the Real Ground," and Jillian Walliss, "Ecology, Scarcity, and the Global South," in Frederick Steiner et. al. (eds), *Design with Nature Now* (Lincoln Institute of Land Policy, 2019).

14. Desimini & Waldheim, *Cartographic Grounds*, 9.

15. "Sea Level Rise Viewer," NOAA, https://coast.noaa.gov/slr/.

16. NOAA's Sea Level Rise View is also of limited use because it does not take into account rainfall quantity, intensity, and inland flooding, which are now and in the near future far more important considerations than is sea level rise for most locations.

17. Latour, "Anti-zoom," 121. Other critiques of "Powers of Ten" can be found in Tong, "Ecology without Scale"; Schneider & Walsh, "The Politics of Zoom"; and Derek Woods, "Scale Critique for the Anthropocene," *Minnesota Review* 83 (2014): 133–42.

18. Clark, "Scale," 148; Sutherland, "Mapping

the Space of Flows," 193.

19. For a recent discussion on these references to Haraway and Pickles see Heather Houser, *Infowhelm: Environmental Art and Literature in an Age of Data* (Columbia University Press, 2020), 198, 202. On the employment of these techniques in landscape architecture, see James Corner & Alex S. MacLean, *Taking Measures Across the American Landscape* (Yale University Press, 1996) and Anuradha Mathur & Dilip da Cunha, *Mississippi Floods: Designing a Shifting Landscape* (Yale University Press, 2001).

20. Jeremy W. Crampton & John Krygier, "An Introduction to Critical Cartography," *ACME: An International E-Journal for Critical Geographies* 4, no 1 (2006): 18.

21. Desimini & Waldheim, *Cartographic Grounds*, 10.

22. Ibid.

23. Karl Kullman, "The Satellites' Progeny: Digital Chorography in the Age of Drone Vision," *Forty-Five* 3 (2017).

24. On the third and fourth shorelines, Monmonier states: "Heavily dependent on numerical modeling and evolving scientific understanding of physical processes, these two new land-water boundaries exemplify the emergence of time as a cartographic frontier in the nineteenth and twentieth centuries, when earth system forecasting became an important mapping application." Mark Monmonier (ed.), *The History of Cartography Volume 6: Cartography in the Twentieth Century* (University of Chicago Press, 2015), 238–39. Also see Mark Monmonier, *Coastlines: How Map Makers Frame the World and Chart Environmental Change* (University of Chicago Press, 2008).

25. Ellipsoid and geoid datums differ in that the former is a simplified geometric model of earth's surface while the latter is determined using the earth's gravitational force plus one or two local tide gauges. The distance between the geoid and a specific place on the Earth is called orthometric height, which are the elevations labeled on a contour map. Without a vertical datum, ellipsoidal heights cannot be converted to orthometric elevations.

26. See entry "My handheld GPS gives me bad elevations. Why?" USACE, https://www.mvn.usace.army.mil/Missions/Engineering/Survey-Section/FAQ/.

27. P.M. Bartier & N.A. Sloan, "Reconciling Maps with Charts towards Harmonizing Coastal Zone Base Mapping: A Case Study from British Columbia," *Journal of Coastal Research* 23, no. 1 (2007): 75–86.

28. Blue-green bathymetric lidar can "see" past the surface of the water but only in shallow areas of clear water and thus is largely ineffective in turbid waters, such as streams, rivers, and oceans.

29. B. Parker, et al., "A Tampa Bay bathymetric/topographic digital elevation model with internally consistent shorelines for various datums," *Proceedings of the Twelfth Biennial International Symposium of the Hydrographic Society*, University of East Anglia, Norwich, UK (2001).

30. As stated in the 2006 report by the US Army Corps of Engineers, "Performance Evaluation of the New Orleans and Southeast Louisiana Hurricane Protection System Volume 1 Executive Summary and Overview" (USACE, 2006) I-5, I-7.

31. Oliver E. Wing, et al., "Estimates of Present and Future Flood Risk in the Conterminous United States," *Environmental Research Letters* 13 (2018). On the significance of this for landscape architecture, see Karen M'Closkey & Keith VanDerSys, "For Whom Do We Account in Climate Adaptation?" in Carolyn Kousky, Billy Fleming & Alan M. Berger (eds), *A Blueprint for Coastal Adaptation: Uniting Design, Economics, and Policy* (Island Press, 2021).

32. Hamed R. Moftakhari, et al., "What is Nuisance Flooding? Defining and Monitoring an Emerging Challenge," *Water Resources Research* 54 (2018), 4218–27.

33. As Matthew Wilson writes, "there are limits to relying on 1980s–1990s critical perspectives on GIS and mapping for unpacking our contemporary moment." Matthew Wilson, *New Lines: Critical GIS and the Trouble of the Map* (University of Minnesota Press, 2017), 26. Robert Pietrusko similarly argues that those critiques "communicated a belief that cartographic projects at the scale of contemporary environmental concerns—potentially involving a large community of experts—were impossible to execute ethically." Pietrusko, "A Speculative Cartography," in Benjamin H. Bratton, et al., eds. *The New Normal* (University of Chicago Press, 2021), 129.

DRAWING

Valerio Morabito

Valerio Morabito is a professor at the Mediterranean University in Italy, and a former adjunct professor at the University of Pennsylvania Weitzman School of Design. He is founding principal of the design firm APScape, whose work includes the Garden of Cultural Heritage, which won the silver medal at the International Horticultural Expo 2021 in Yangzhou, China. His recent book *The City of Imagination* (2020) is a collection of more than 150 drawings imagining cities worldwide.

As an Italian architect writing a text in English about the role of drawing in landscape architecture, a short preamble is necessary to establish the commonalities and differences between the English word "drawing" and the Italian equivalent, *"disegno."* If we compare the *English Oxford Dictionary* definition of drawing with the *Italian Garzanti Dictionary* definition of *disegno*, important differences can be identified. The *Oxford Dictionary* explains that drawing as a verb means the art or activity of making drawings, and as a noun it refers to a picture or diagram made with a pencil, pen, charcoal, or crayon rather than paint. The *Garzanti Dictionary*, on the other hand, sets out at least six potential meanings for the Italian equivalent, including the representation of things through lines and signs; the art of drawing; the model or study for the realization of something; an ornamental pattern; an outline or draft; and a plan, purpose, or intention. In English, then, drawing's relationship with art is not clearly enunciated whereas in the Italian definition it is. In English, drawing is also an action—drawing is the gerund of the verb to draw—whereas *disegno* is not an action – its gerund is *disegnando*. Most importantly, in Italian *disegno* means not just to draw things, but to design them – an example given is God's divine plan, no less.

God's design for life aside, when I think of drawing I think of *disegno*. But for me its definition still falls short of the actual creative potential of drawing. The drawing, therefore, that I would like to "draw" attention to is a tool that supports imagination and creativity for testing conceptual ideas and innovative design methodologies. This type of drawing doesn't just record impressions, it generates thoughts, from analysis to design. Through drawing one reflects on ideas, speculates on spaces and places, and creates utopian and dystopian scenarios. The challenge, of course, is to make drawings that are as evocative as I am suggesting they can be. This has something to do with striking a balance between figure and void, between areas of information and white space, leaving margins, and knowing when a drawing is complete, or rather sufficiently incomplete and intentionally imperfect. The following notes are a sketch of my ideal drawing.

White spaces—voids on the page—are fundamental to the composition of a drawing. They produce rhythms, structure of narrative, hierarchies, and relationships between elements helping to configure the drawing as a text to be read or a kind of musical notation to be imagined. White space serves to breathe a lightness into drawings. One of the clearest and most significant examples of this can be found in traditional Chinese landscape painting – an artistic expression that is not only a description of the visible world, but also the invisible. The use of voids and lightness convey the artist's perception of how energy and spirit move through the world, transforming mere representations into idealized images. For more contemporary examples we can turn to the early-20th-century artistic movement Dada, which gave rise to representation as a form of psychogeography. Using random words different in scale, shapes, and character, artists displayed them casually on the paper, achieving a sense of lightness combined with a sense of beauty and immediacy.

Margins perform a similar role, allowing readers space to add their own thoughts to a drawing's narrative. John Dixon Hunt has written about the necessity of margins in contemporary design, leaving space for others to add their own notes in much the same way that readers notate the pages of books.[1] The use of white space and margins help make drawings operate as "open frameworks," a concept borrowed from Umberto Eco's idea of "open work."[2] Eco declared that a work of art is not a conclusive experience. He explained that a work of art has an aesthetic value when it catalyzes different interpretations of it. Lawrence Halprin's Grand Canyon natural landscape drawings are examples of open frameworks, leaving white spaces and margins. His sketches, notes, and memories were used to create events in the design of public spaces.

Intentional imperfection is important in a drawing because it keeps the drawing open. If a drawing is perfect it has no chance of life beyond itself, it is not open to evolution. The universe was born imperfect and asymmetric in shapes and forces. It is through this small degree of imperfection that life's constant creativity emerges. Evolutionary processes are unpredictable because the previous stages of systems are necessary but not sufficient to predict future steps in advance. Future states of the system are randomly dependent on former states. The mode of drawing I am interested in taps into this indeterminacy in a quest for originality.

To explain the role of originality, it is necessary to refer to Walter Benjamin's 1935 essay "The Work of Art in the Age of Mechanical Reproduction," and, in particular, to his concepts of concentration and distraction. A traditional work of art such as a painting or a sculpture, Benjamin argued, needs concentration to be perceived by the individual observer. Consequently, the observer is absorbed by the work of art, becoming part of it. The more the observer concentrates, the more the observer is absorbed by the work of art.[3] In contrast, he noted, photographs and movies require less concentration and are generally received by mass audiences who share their responses to the work. The audience members are not absorbed by the work, rather they absorb it.[4] Benjamin argues that architecture also functions in this manner and, if so, then this is even more valid for landscape architecture because parks, gardens, and public spaces are places used by masses of people that perceive them through a distracted attitude of shared pleasure and disinterest.

However, Benjamin fails to consider that works of landscape architecture and architecture typically have two moments of perception by an observer: one related to the project's representation in drawing, and the other following its physical realization. Yves Brunier was perhaps one of the first landscape architects to communicate to a mass audience through the originality of his drawings. Benjamin says that the originality of a work of art maintains an aura well recognizable because it is easy to place it in time and space, recognizing its uniqueness. It could be added that the originality of the contemporary landscape architecture drawing is also given by its ability to survive the project for which it was designed: whether the project was realized or not. An iconic example of this kind of originality in the passage between analog and digital techniques is the drawings produced by OMA for the design competition for the Park de La Villette in Paris. Even though the OMA project did not win the competition, the drawings were able to spread an idea of the landscape as a process, not a picture-perfect parkland. Those drawings survived the competition, and they are still examples of how to imagine and create new ideas; in the end, they maintained their originality. For me, then, the landscape project lies first and foremost with the act of drawing; drawing that imperfectly circumscribes the edges of voids, openings, and margins.

1. John Dixon Hunt, "Sette lezioni sul paesaggio," trans. Valerio Morabito, *Liberia Edizioni* (2013).

2. Eco Umberto, *Open Work* (Bompiani Editore, 1968).

3. Walter Benjamin, "The Work of Art in the Age of Mechanical Reproduction (1935)," reproduced in Hannah Arendt (ed.), *Illuminations* (Schocken Books, 1969).

4. Ibid.

PRACTICE

Lucinda Sanders

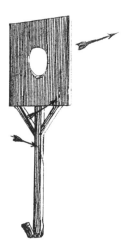

Lucinda Sanders is a design partner and the president and CEO of OLIN, and is an adjunct professor at the University of Pennsylvania Weitzman School of Design. Fueled by the belief that transforming thinking transforms place, Lucinda has led many of OLIN's signature projects and cofounded OLIN LABS, the studio's in-house research practice. Beyond OLIN, she serves on boards and in academia dedicated to the advancement of landscape architecture, and co-facilitates the Landscape Architecture Foundation's Fellowship for Innovation and Leadership.

While I write primarily from the perspective of practice, my affiliation with academia allows me to view the profession holistically. I frequently witness a seeming disconnect between practice and the academy. What the landscape project has been and is in practice, and the possibilities that the academy often project onto the profession, can leave practitioners wondering if the academy understands what is needed to bring a project to fruition and the academy wondering why many practitioners, and the institutions that represent those practitioners, are slow to catch on to contemporary ideas and are apparently lethargic when it comes to advocacy. I firmly believe this discomfiting tension, when embraced, is an energy that can and should propel both the profession and practice, forward.

In this essay I examine some key characteristics of what it means to be a landscape architect and situate the profession alongside others. Acknowledging that practice is a joyful and creative enterprise satisfying many impulses shared by landscape architects, we need to be honest; our claims that we shape human society for the better because of our understanding of the biotic and abiotic worlds is limited to a very small portion of the earth's surface. I expose the conundrum of devoting resources and energy to practice and simultaneously making important professional advancements beyond the borders of any one project. My aim is to elucidate the possibilities—and obstacles—faced by landscape architects, enhance personal and professional efficacy, and, for students, help to direct and forge exciting and rewarding careers shaping and evolving the profession.

Many landscape architects are ambitious, holistic thinkers. We, along with a handful of other people, seem to be wired this way. This is an observation corroborated by my research conducted between 2013 and 2018 on transformational leadership, an idea that is distinct from transactional leadership.[1] More specifically, in my research, I sought to understand the inner workings of people who had demonstrated interest in bringing about transformations to make a healthier, more just, and equitable future, essentially the creation of a "do no harm" future. These are people, regardless of positional power who, as it turns out, operate from a source quite distinct from transactional leaders. I interviewed people across a spectrum of ages and professions—community leaders, activists, artists, authors, academics, students, lawyers, politicians, and, yes, landscape architects—who demonstrated evidence of transformational leadership. I was interested to learn what they were thinking, sensing, and feeling in the process of bringing about transformation. Here is what I discovered:

- They generally believe in an ethical future – one in which peaceful and large-scale societal and environmental change will take place for the greater good.

- They possess a quantum worldview, a worldview with roots in physics that broadly accepts the interconnected nature of everything, even if it cannot yet be fully explained. This worldview is distinct from a Newtonian worldview which explains the world primarily through isolation of elements or cause and effect.

- They view transformation as the unfoldment of life and not a distinct moment in time with a beginning, middle, and end. It's not a project or an event. It is a life calling, a way of thinking about and being in the world.

- They believe in the worthiness of all humans, which transcends differences and elicits empathy.

- While there are struggles with the ego, these individuals are typically not motivated by power plays, but rather by supporting the greater good.

My concern as the CEO of OLIN, a teacher, and an active supporter of the Landscape Architecture Foundation is how these values translate into practice. Because something else that comes through in my interactions with landscape architects is that they are often frustrated by a sense that the world doesn't share their worldview, and they often feel incapacitated to effect meaningful and timely change. So, what's stopping them?

Let's start with the size of the profession. The 2020 United States labor force statistics reveal that the number of landscape architects employed in the US is under 25,000. When we compare ourselves to other professions in the 2020 US labor force—architects (~126,000), civil engineers (~309,000), physicians and surgeons (~727,000), and lawyers (~804,000)—we are a miniscule profession.[2] Worldwide, our numbers are not much better. Although the number is difficult to track with complete accuracy, according to the International Federation of Landscape Architects, landscape architects worldwide numbered approximately 35,000 in 2017. Clearly our momentum as a profession is challenged by our capacity. Similarly, the areas of land we actually work on are often diminutive in relation to the scale of the looming contemporary environmental and social problems.

Further complicating matters, we need to understand the reality that most landscape architects work outside of government agencies in private practice, which belongs to a larger umbrella category known as professional service firms (PSF).[3] The foundation of a PSF is to provide customized knowledge-based services to our clients. Not to be understated, clients usually seek our services once the focus and intention of a project has already been established. This raises the question: is the landscape project in practice possibly circumscribed by clients thereby blunting broader tendencies and ambitions harbored by landscape architects? The answer is, partially.

Finally, the formalization of the relationship with the client into a contract, which also defines the fees for services, adds further constrictions. I call this the transactional side of practice and sometimes it can pull us away from the transformational. Taken together, these phenomena seem to silence the once audible voices of students and undermine the idealized visions developed in the academy. This process of inurement is partially responsible for the characterization of landscape architects as a shade-loving species; but, with enough intention, we do not have to succumb to those forces that compromise our potential potency.

Comprehending the transformational–transactional spectrum of our profession and how it relates to leadership can help. If we think of the possibility for ethically motivated transformation as a wedge from low to high, design thinking in advanced landscape studios in the academy is ambitious in its subject matter and projective in its resolution: the work usually aspires to be transformational in vitally important ways. I would argue that studio work, at least here in the Weitzman School of Design, sits far to the right in this spectrum. While there is room for invention and innovation, practice has rules and requires levels of efficiency that often limit the potential for transformation, constricting the profession's breadth, depth, and efficacy. This transactional force operates in opposition to the transformational wedge. Purely transactional relationships often arise out of positional power. The more transactional a relationship is, the more it squeezes out the possibility for ethically based transformation to occur. But fortunately, the world is rarely so binary. As I will show, within reason, there are ways to make the transactional transformative.

Most relationships with clients are a balance of these two forces. How a practice thinks about this balance and maneuvers in this territory is crucial to determining its identity and its mission. This position is an indicator of the culture and projected longevity of that practice and is a gauge of its transformational potential. Taken together, the zone of the

landscape project is a wide band that incorporates academia and practice. The transformational visioning work that takes place in academic studios is vitally important and the work translating ideas and theory on the ground is also essential to make ideas real.[4] I believe the landscape project resides not merely in responsively producing ethical and high-quality work—that is a baseline condition—it is in guiding the profession forward through uncharted terrain. Of particular interest to me is the zone in between, in the gap, where practice evolves, where research and invention happen, where innovation occurs, and where the spirit of optimism is renewed. These are the activities that stretch practice and thereby the profession.

What does one need to do to work in the gap? While each designer may attempt to be as ethical and conscientious as possible, we have to first admit that there is a disconnect in the output of practice and our ability to answer the criticisms that we are not acting at the scale of the crises at hand, and that we often fail to satisfy the rhetoric of our various declarations and mission statements. Only when we admit these shortcomings can we effectively address them. We must stop believing that this small band of landscape architects are the only ones who are prescient and can solve these looming issues. We need to recognize that we are not alone – we have colleagues and collaborators and we must become increasingly proficient in working with them. We must recognize that our work is not neutral. To work in any landscape is value laden, deeply political, and nested within larger scales of influence and impact. To be effective, we must be willing to engage these systems and, when necessary, step outside of traditional professional boundaries. Practitioners who are called to answer the crisis at scale will need to develop different practice models and not wait for the as yet unidentified clients to emerge if they are to insert themselves into these territories. Think, for example, of the entrenched and highly regulated nature of the agricultural industries that make intervention in this vast and important landscape presently out of reach of mainstream practice. The same is true of the landscapes of energy. Yet in both instances, increasingly I work with landscape architects who are anxious to be more effective at tackling these topics.

Some academics, firms, and nonprofits manage to practice to great effect in the gap, but one thing I have observed is that those who choose to work in the gap usually do so from the relatively secure footing of the academy, traditional practice, or by procuring an amalgam of funding sources. Although at OLIN we remain squarely within a service provision model of project delivery we have been able to create a culture within the practice that supports the study of urgent needs and transformative aspiration. We have done this by underwriting research and development on our projects through OLIN Labs,[5] a distinctly cultural decision on allocation of profit, which is not a model readily adopted by many practices. I have also chosen to use the foundation of teaching at the Weitzman School of Design to introduce concepts of transformational leadership to students of landscape architecture with the intention to set them on a productive path to develop a voice that can be heard above the din of naysayers.

This is an idea that transcends the traditional tenets of professional practice. I desperately want graduates to understand that if they aspire to bring about much-needed change beyond project boundaries, they will need to comprehend the parameters of the profession, muster the courage to show up differently from their predecessors, and be willing to dig deeply into terrain that may be unfamiliar. They need to learn to identify points and places of leverage, which are most likely not found in a traditional practice. And, most importantly, they will need to carve out the time and space to work on transformations, as most practices are not petri dishes waiting for the next invention. The richness of the landscape project in practice can be found by mining the tensions in the fertile ground of the gap and by holding true to our vision of a better world. This could become a new ethical tenet of practice. We must not settle for anything less.

1. Aspects of these theories took root in the 1970s when James McGregor Burns described transactional and transforming leadership, and were augmented in the 1980s by Bernard Bass who coined the term transformational leadership. Over the last quarter century, these theories were deepened by a cadre of researchers from MIT including Peter Senge, William Isaacs, and C. Otto Scharmer.

2. US Bureau of Labor Statistics, *Occupational Outlook Handbook 2020*, https://www.bls.gov/ooh (retrieved November 8, 2021).

3. Of the member base of the American Society of Landscape Architects (ASLA) nearly 70% are in some form of practice. The ASLA statistics do not capture professional affiliations of non-members nor do they reflect the international community.

4. Here I would be remiss if I did not mention professional organizations (ASLA, CELA, LAAC, CLARB) and nonprofits (LAF, TCLF, and the more recent BlackLAN and The Urban Studio) that play a sometimes-unwitting role in defining the scope of the landscape project, as they either advance or suppress the rate of evolution of practice and the academy depending on the leadership of each organization.

5. OLIN Labs, https://olinlabs.com/.

PURPOSE

Rebecca Popowsky & Sarai Williams

Rebecca Popowsky is a landscape architect and research associate at OLIN, where she leads the firm's research and development group, OLIN Labs. Her research includes waste-based material design and practice-based research models. Rebecca teaches core and advanced design studios at the University of Pennsylvania Weitzman School of Design, including a seminar (with Sarai Williams) that explores purpose in landscape architectural practice.

Sarai Williams is on the social impact real estate team for Community Solutions, a national nonprofit working with cities to create a lasting end to homelessness. Her work centers around adapting housing systems to be more equitable and comprehensively supportive to society's most vulnerable populations.

The widening gap between the changes that *must* be made in the built environment and those that *can* be made through conventional models of professional design practice is driving a generation of landscape architects, architects, and planners to search out and create new modes of practice. In this essay, we describe aspects of this emergence within the current structures of professional landscape architectural practice and discuss several landscape architecture and planning practices that present potential to expand the scope, and in some cases, challenge the foundations of these existing structures.

To paint a clear picture of current professional landscape architectural practice, it may be helpful first to describe an analogous professional services model that is more widely familiar – that of law, which has well-established models for public interest practice. Law school prepares would-be lawyers to analyze and apply statutes, regulations, and case law, but generally does not prepare students to become agents of social good. However, the profession has addressed the need to put the law to positive use by creating public interest and government practice models, giving practicing lawyers the opportunity—or obligation—to handle pro bono cases. Non-governmental public interest lawyers who work for groups like the National Association for the Advancement of Colored People (NAACP) and the American Civil Liberties Union (ACLU) work to advance societal goals and are generally supported by public and private grants and private donations.

In comparison, the landscape architecture profession has a very small government sector, almost no pro bono mechanism, and no formal public interest sector at all. One obvious reason for this difference is the relative size of the profession – while there are about 800,000 licensed attorneys in the US, the Department of Labor estimates the number of professional landscape architects to be under 25,000. Another reason is that landscape architects haven't effectively communicated the societal value of the profession to the general public, so little public and philanthropic funding is directed to landscape architectural services. While legal services are widely seen as critical to the protection of individual and community rights, design services (especially in landscape) are more often seen as an unnecessary luxury. However, when the impact of the design of the built environment on issues of social justice and public health is appreciated—especially in a time of extreme climate change and widening inequality—the landscape project should be recognized as an essential service. Absent a source of substantial funding for public interest landscape architecture, landscape architects must themselves build a structure that allows this essential service to be advanced within or alongside the existing practice model.

While comparison to analogous fields such as law is helpful, it is important to draw some distinctions that might otherwise be overlooked. One is the distinction between pro bono work and public interest work. State bars set minimum pro bono (or unpaid work) requirements for lawyers, embedding a measure of social obligation into the legal profession. While this certainly has a positive impact at scale (and is something the Council of Landscape Architectural Registration Boards—the licensing body for landscape architects—should consider implementing), pro bono work within private practice generally cannot make serious headway on complex societal or environmental problems. In contrast, public interest legal organizations, such as the NAACP or the ACLU, which support full-time professionals and are expressly established for this purpose, play a significant role in delineation of fundamental civil rights. In this essay, we will refer to both pro bono and public interest work as "purpose-driven" work. This term is used in contrast to "profit-driven" to indicate that the primary goal of a project or practice is societal or environmental benefit rather than private economic gain.

A similar distinction should be made between overhead and overtime. In the absence of substantial public interest design funding, purpose-driven work is often non-billable, unfunded, or under-funded. In order for an individual practitioner to take on unfunded work, they may need to perform the work outside of "work hours," that is, at night or on the weekends. This can be considered *overtime*. If, on the other hand, a design firm decides to take on non-billable public interest work, that work may be completed during work hours and the cost to the firm can be considered *overhead*. The key difference is that overhead cuts into profit, while overtime cuts into employee or individual personal time. The scale of work that can be done using either overhead or overtime is limited by the budgetary and time constraints of practices and individual practitioners. To push beyond these limits, external funding is required.

Architecture and landscape architecture, like law, are service professions. Design services are commissioned by clients, within a defined scope, for a fee. Design commissions (usually referred to as projects) typically present themselves to design professionals as Requests for Proposals (RFPs). RFPs are issued when three puzzle pieces come together: first, recognition of a need or demand for a built project; second, funding for planning, design, and construction; and third, an individual or number of individuals who have the power and authority to implement the project. When these factors align in a location (project site) an RFP is issued and a design professional can be commissioned to articulate a material form that meets the needs of the project within constraints defined by funding, site, and political, social, and ecological contexts. This model, which might be called the design-commission model, the RFP model, or the client-driven model, can lead to immensely successful built work that provides equitable social, environmental, and economic benefits. However, the good that comes out of any given project depends more on the political, social, and economic context and forces that pre-date the RFP, than on the resulting design actions. In other words, by the time the designer is hired, the overarching impact of the project is largely already set.

To subvert the conventional role of the designer in this design-commission model, projects need to be instigated in the absence of an RFP. Sometimes this means that no client exists; other times a client group has identified a project need, but they do not have access to funding or decision-making authority; in other cases, needs or problems exist on a site but they have not yet been clearly articulated. Practitioners are experimenting with several mechanisms to support project instigation outside of RFP or client-driven scenarios. For example, grant funding, pilot projects, and "communities of practice" support important work outside of, or in addition to, traditional project models. The following cases are helpful in exploring how these mechanisms interface with projects and communities.

Public and philanthropic funding mechanisms such as grants and fellowships are commonly used by designers to support purpose-driven work. Innovative firms have honed their ability to seek out and secure research or seed grants, often in collaboration with academic or institutional partners to support design research and action. Mahan Rykiel Associates, a landscape architecture practice based in Baltimore, for example, has initiated a series of research-based projects around beneficial reuse of dredge material in the Chesapeake Bay, with grant funding from the Maryland Department of Transportation and the Maryland Port Administration and in partnership with researchers at Cornell and the University of Maryland Center for Environmental Science. Outcomes of this research-based initiative have included public engagement and education workshops, experimental seed germination studies, and a site-specific pilot installation, all aimed at reimagining Baltimore Harbor sediment as an essential resource, rather than a waste material. As in this example, grant-funded work often builds upon itself, moving from "proof of concept" research to small-scale pilot installation, and eventually to large-scale implementation.

Merritt Chase, a young practice cofounded by Nina Chase and Chris Merritt, has honed a capacity to move a design agenda forward using pilot-based advocacy projects. They make the case for public space as the foundational building blocks of communities, and for landscape architects to occupy a seat at the table "further upstream" in the process of planning for change (prior to the issuance of the RFP). This compels them to focus much of their attention on short-term design-build projects that aim to build momentum for design ideas. Their "tactical urbanism" projects are about making things that build enthusiasm for longer term investment in the urban landscape. For example, Birch Street Plaza, in Boston's Roslindale Village, which turns a trafficked street into a pedestrian plaza, began as a six-day pop-up plaza that prototyped and tested design elements using duct tape, milk crates, and wooden dowels.

In this case, the pilot project was used largely as a community engagement mechanism that facilitated in-person and online surveys, observation, and conversation that shaped the final plaza design.

Sponge Park on the Gowanus Canal, designed by DLANDstudio is another example of a small-scale pilot project that is intended to pave the way for large-scale transformation. The park is a modular street-end installation that intercepts and filters stormwater while providing accessible neighborhood green space. DLAND worked with the Gowanus Canal Conservancy to pull together funders and public agencies over a multi-year process to get the $1.5 million demonstration project implemented. The pilot project demonstrates the effectiveness of nature-based stormwater management and aims to garner public support for large-scale transformation along the full length of the canal.

While each of these firms found creative ways to leverage alternative funding mechanisms to instigate built projects, another practice, Kounkuey Design Initiative (KDI), used similar mechanisms to support research into building innovative business models. Seed funding allowed the firm's founding members to explore mission-based business models in other fields, before establishing KDI as a non-profit design firm. Based in Los Angeles and Nairobi, KDI balances grant-funded work with traditional client commissions and a small amount of donor funding. The practice model includes hiring local experts in various fields, including design, engineering, and construction, locally, for projects in Africa and the US while serving communities that lack political and economic clout. In this instance, the structure of the firm is as innovative as their design work.

In our research interviewing several of these innovative practitioners, common themes emerged. Practitioners are looking for ways to bring new voices to the table at all stages of the design process; if the people most in need of design services cannot participate substantively in the process, the process will not be fair or just. Practitioners are also looking for ways to ensure that the voices heard within the profession reflect the communities the projects are meant to serve; otherwise, projects will not fully meet community needs. Specifically, community input must be more than obligatory steps taken to smooth the way for development, or for the superimposition of a single designer's vision. Opening the design process to multiple voices and reorienting design services toward communities in need represents a paradigm shift in contemporary design culture. To support this type of community-oriented work, landscape architects must take advantage of alternative funding mechanisms and collaborative structures.

Another common sentiment among these practitioners is that working outside of the typical client-commissioned design model adds layers of complexity and cost that are borne by firms and individual practitioners. They talk about the need to be open to "failing forward"; in other words, missteps are part of the process and should be seen as opportunities to reexamine approaches or refine or adapt objectives. Leaving established professional structures behind is an unruly and risky business. Practitioners are compelled to establish new structures to support their work, while also providing design services. As a community, we can do more to collectively support this kind of work through education and skill-building and by building networks of support among practitioners.

In addition to non-traditional funding mechanisms, purpose-driven work can be supported by formal or informal social infrastructures that make space for open-ended collaboration and design exploration. "Communities of practice" (CoP) were defined in the 1990s by educational theorist Etienne Wenger as "a group of people who share a concern, a set of problems, or a passion about a topic, and who deepen their knowledge and expertise in this area by interacting on an ongoing basis."[1] The CoP model is different from a typical professional organization or institution, in that involvement is voluntary and not project- or profit-oriented. Communities of practice are commonly housed within businesses, though they can also function outside of (or bridge across) formal institutions. While big corporations like Ford and IBM use the model as a formal platform for innovation, problem-solving, and driving change, this type of social infrastructure is not often discussed in the design industry.

OLIN Labs is an example of the community of practice model housed within a private firm. Five topic-based "Labs" (Eco, Build, Tech, People, and Design) host regular meetings among designers at all levels across the firm in conversation around topics of shared interest. This model, which is internally funded and relies on voluntary staff participation, creates space within the workday for designers to identify research and design projects outside of the RFP pipeline, and work together with colleagues and external collaborators to find creative ways to bring those projects into being. Discussions that grow out of the Labs' communities of practice sometimes turn into opportunities for informal learning, and other times become freestanding research or advocacy initiatives or pilot projects that can attract grant or client funding. The belief here is that robust communities of practice may offer routes to purpose-driven and impactful design action.

Other examples include WxLA and The Urban Studio. WxLA, organized by Gina Ford, Jamie Maslyn Larson, Rebecca Leonard, and Cinda Gilliland, is not firm- or project-specific (Ford, Larson, Leonard, and Gilliland all run their own firms) but brings practitioners together around the goal of gender equality in the profession. Initiatives, such as the WxLA annual scholarships, grow out of this shared mission and community-based infrastructure. The Urban Studio initially arose from a collaboration among Landscape Architecture Foundation Leadership and Innovation Fellows and then grew into a team of practitioners organized around a shared cause, bridging firms, that, in addition to paid consulting work, take on co-design and co-creation workshops in communities of color. In contrast to the traditional for-profit design firm model, The Urban Studio exists primarily as a platform for collaboration among professionals. They convene industry-wide conversations through their annual Cut/Fill "un-conference," relying on donor funding from mission-aligned design firms and industry partners. The studio also brings together practitioners from other firms to take part in career discovery workshops in underserved communities. In both instances, communities of practice provide social infrastructures that challenge the profession to more equitably reflect and represent the populations that we serve.

Skills that would facilitate non-conventional practice scenarios such as grant-writing, community organizing, research methods, policy analysis, and business planning, are not generally considered central to design curricula. At some schools, students have the chance to learn these skills by taking part in public-interest work through university-backed centers that hire students as researchers or designers either during the school year or over the summer. Upon graduation, however, emerging design practitioners tend to perceive their career path as one they walk alone. Visual artists are accustomed to the idea that attracting an audience and building collaborative platforms through which their art will be displayed, are as critical to successful practice as the production of art. Artists, who have to not only invent their own projects but then find ways to fund them, hone skills in grant writing and pitching projects to potential patrons, searching for seed funding while communicating their ideas on multiple levels so as to build their reputations as emerging practitioners. If design education is to support emerging forms of practice, a similar set of skills will need to be foregrounded. Even as individual firms and practitioners are finding creative ways to reimagine professional practice models, the field of landscape architecture currently lacks sufficient shared infrastructure to support industry-wide transformation. Rather, efforts to challenge the conventional role of design are ad hoc and rely heavily on voluntary sacrifice on the part of firms and practitioners through non-billable overhead or unpaid overtime.

Frustration among practitioners, students, and academics with the limitations of professional landscape architectural practice is high. If we're honest with ourselves, we would likely find that the great majority of landscape architects would prefer to work in public-interest scenarios, rather than on projects that primarily support private interests. The problem is that the field lacks robust professional structures that make this type of work sustainable at scale over the long term. Practitioners who are actively trying to get purpose-driven work done (outside of university or government structures) are faced with the difficult task of building the stage that they are performing on, while convincing a non-existent audience to show up and pay attention. Landscape architecture, like architecture, is a very challenging profession even for those practitioners who "just" work on conventional design commissions. Doing anything even slightly outside of that realm is even more difficult, and it can be risky (professionally and financially) without robust support structures. Current and future landscape architectural practices will need to take on the unruly challenge of building these structures cooperatively, if we want to be relevant in the coming decades. To help achieve this we can look to practical precedents such as formalizing a pro-bono system in landscape architecture, building our capacity in government, and also more seriously considering the way in which artists and the not-for-profit sector invent, promote, and build coalitions for their projects.

1. Etienne Wenger, Richard A. McDermott & William Snyder, *Cultivating Communities of Practice: A guide to managing knowledge* (Harvard Business Press, 2002).

POLITICS

Billy Fleming

Billy Fleming is the Wilks Family Director of the Ian L. McHarg Center for Urbanism and Ecology at the University of Pennsylvania Weitzman School of Design. He is coeditor of *A Blueprint for Coastal Adaptation* (2021) and *Design with Nature Now* (2019), and coauthor of "The Indivisible Guide." His writing has been published in *Places Journal*, *The Atlantic*, *Dissent Magazine*, *The Guardian*, *Bloomberg*, *Metropolis, Landscape Journal*, *LA+ Journal*, *Architectural Design*, and *Journal of Architectural Education*.

This is the time of crisis. In communities across the world, state and police violence is becoming ever more cruel and brazen; and the roiling heat and flames, surging seas and storms, and stark realities of another great migration unleashed by the climate crisis are fundamentally reshaping how and where we live and relate to each other. At times, these effects are visceral and episodic, thrusting questions of climate justice into the foreground. The aftermaths of Hurricane Maria in Puerto Rico, the collapse of a deregulated electricity grid in Texas, or the violent crackdowns against Indigenous-led protests against lithium mining in the Andean Mountains of Chile are but a few examples of this momentary foregrounding. But more often, the specter of the climate crisis is more difficult to detect. It is the backdrop against which a global network of resurgent, right-wing authoritarians have begun to imagine their own ecotopian futures – ones predicated upon a narrow sense of belonging, rooted in the "blood in soil" nationalism of white supremacy, and committed to the hardened borders and isolationism that has become known as eco-apartheid. Their program is already being piloted in Brazil and a growing cadre of US lawmakers—including Senators Tom Cotton and Marco Rubio—are appending their presidential ambitions to it.[1] Whether through the genocidal nationalism of Brazilian President Jair Bolsonaro or the poll-tested, isolationist "Buy American" rhetoric of US President Joe Biden, the stakes and potential futures of the climate crisis have never been clearer. In a century that will be defined by either international cooperation or competition, the only program currently on the table capable of delivering global climate justice is the Green New Deal.[2]

This stark reality was foretold by Naomi Klein in *This Changes Everything*, in which she writes that "running an economy on energy sources that release poisons as an unavoidable part of their extraction and refining and consumption has always required sacrifice zones – whole subsets of humanity categorized as less than fully human, which made their poisoning in the name of progress somehow acceptable…our political-economic systems and our planetary systems are now at war."[3] To put it more plainly, sacrifice zones tend to be low-income, BIPOC communities in areas either already bearing or expected to bear the brunt of the climate crisis. The Lower Ninth Ward as it relates to New Orleans, Cancer Alley as it relates to the larger Gulf South, and Pacific Island nations as they relate to the Global North each represent different scales of a sacrifice zone. As a set of landscapes and geographic units, this concept of and theory of change within sacrifice zones remains woefully under-developed in landscape architectural scholarship and practice.

As Olufemi Taiwo and Liam Kofi Bright argued in *Dissent*, the time of crisis is an inevitable result of a world organized by global and racial capitalism, governed by the Global North, and powered by fossil fuels.[4] Though it would be easy to dismiss such concerns as orthogonal to aims and operations of design professions, their relationship is more tightly coupled than one might assume. This is, in part, because contrary to the myth-making and triumphalist rhetoric that defines much of design scholarship, the design professions are often indistinguishable in their aims, operations, and outcomes from the rest of the professional services industry. Put another way, the design professions are best understood as materially and conceptually aligned with multi-national consulting firms like McKinsey & Company. While their instruments differ—consulting firms typically focus on organizational structure and optimizing corporate and regime finances, while design firms focus on the built and natural environments—they often pursue commissions and contracts from the same pool of public and private capital, in many of the same cities and nations, and often complicit in some of the most egregious forms of human immiseration that capitalism has to offer. Viewing the fields in this way can help one reconcile otherwise intractable questions like: how is it that a massive, global firm like AECOM can justify building climate adaptation infrastructure *and* prisons?[5] How can a firm like HOK categorize its work as "justice" driven as it too builds prisons *and* designs headquarters and infrastructure for the fossil fuel industry? How can a practice like MSP be viewed as a leader on climate change

at the same time as it develops high-carbon, eco-apartheid luxury projects for autocratic regimes in the Middle East? How can a practitioner like Bjarke Ingels rationalize building some of the century's most celebrated social housing *and* develop eco-tourism projects for a genocidal, authoritarian regime in Brazil?[6] Though its manifestations vary from era-to-era and place-to-place, design tends to go where capital flows.

While design has always found itself tethered to and bounded by political economic frameworks, this chapter is focused on the ways in which contemporary urbanization and capitalism are linked and laundered through the built environment by the design professions. More specifically, this chapter is focused on the design academy in general and the design studio in particular. This is, at least in part, because the academy is one of the few spaces of exception, theoretically insulated from market forces and unencumbered with the kinds of business development practices required to keep private firms running. And the core of nearly all design education is the studio. To do so, I must begin with a simple premise: that design, as currently constituted, is simply not capable of reconciling its ethical and material contradictions – of urban greening and ecological gentrification, of high-carbon luxury real estate development and LEED or SITES certification standards, and of state-led investments in urbanism with state-sanctioned violence. While a program like the Green New Deal cannot solve this problem for the design disciplines, it does provide an invitation to think differently about how their values, alignments, and practices might be reconstituted for a century defined by crises.

The Studio

In the time of upheaval and crisis, what is the point of design education? In nearly every school of architecture or design in the US, there is a central, unspoken rejoinder to this question: the point of design education is to condition each successive generation of students for a lifetime of exploited labor that is detached from any critical relationship to the role that designers play in aestheticizing and instrumentalizing global capitalism. While there are always spaces of exception in the academy—the long tradition of community-engaged studios (e.g., Auburn University's Rural Studio, the University of Pennsylvania's nascent Studio+, and a number of design-build studios elsewhere), most efforts tend to reproduce the long hours and infinite production that links design education and practice. This goal is not written in mission statements or strategic plans – to do so would threaten the machinery of student recruitment and major gift fundraising. But it is there, plain to see, in the tendency of design institutions to valorize individuality and competition, endless work, and service to the elites that fund much of the field's work. Design education often exists to reproduce the social and racial order of capitalism. And the core of its pedagogy is the studio.

This is hardly a novel analysis. Peggy Deamer deftly recognizes this relationship in *Architecture and Capitalism: 1845 to the Present*, writing that "while the construction industry participates energetically in the economic engine that is the base [of design practice], architecture operates in the realm of culture, allowing capital to do its work without its effects being scrutinized."[7] Douglas Spencer gestures in this direction in *The Architecture of Neoliberalism*, writing that "while architects and architectural theorists have generally been less brazen (than Schumacher) about their enthusiasms for the subsumption of the urban and architectural orders to those of the market, they have tended, since the mid-1990s in particular, to push those same truths of the way of the world as have served [the logic] of neoliberalism."[8] This, borrowing from Fisher's theory of capitalist realism, situates the design fields alongside the rest of the professional services industry in finding it "easier to imagine an end to civilization than an end to capitalism."[9] In this reading of design culture, our professions are not exceptional or unique – they are simply bound or boxed-in by the political economies of urbanization.

Yet, the studio is rarely imagined in such nefarious terms. Quite the contrary – many, if not most, studio critics are working in earnest to train their students to build a variety of skills, whether organized around technical expertise or critical thinking and analysis. It would be rare and quite shocking to see any curriculum overtly embrace the sorts of norms or culture outlined above. But this analysis is rooted less in overt proclamations and more in the kinds of knowledge production valorized within the design academy – one in which few challenge the supremacy or naturalization of markets. Fewer still take seriously the work of Black Marxists around sacrifice zones – the conceptual framework that racial capitalism requires sacrifice zones, that those zones are delineated in time and space by existing and imagined racial hierarchies, and that those spatial and temporal patterns repeat within and across communities, cities, and regions.[10] While their efforts are surely important, they are no match for the power of an institution—especially elite institutions—to, by and large, manage capital and reproduce the status quo.[11] For all of landscape architecture's, architecture's, and city planning's self-referential talk about imagination and creativity, much of its praxis is organized around themes of aesthetic or formalist experimentation, techno-futurism aligned with the aims of Silicon Valley, and the elite-led sects of the environmental movement often replete with Malthusian undertones of overpopulation, and then filtered through capitalist realism that masquerades as a kind of realpolitik – despite the total lack of political education within the fields.

Alternative Presents

Rather than engaging in this form of critique solely for the sake of critique, or proposing a series of naïve solutions to a set of problems that are ultimately larger than and unsolvable by design, what I'd prefer to do is point toward alternatives. In this case, those alternatives, channeled through a studio sequence known as "Designing a Green New Deal" (DGND), have sought to build new alignments with the climate justice movement and the built environment professions. Rob Holmes opens up this kind of praxis in novel ways, arguing that "there is a methodological tendency, a way of doing the work of making landscapes and infrastructure, that contributes to this cycle of self-defeat [in landscape architecture]…solutionism doesn't know what to do with [complex] landscapes like this, and it leaves us in the unsatisfactory bind of either reducing landscape complexities to solvable problems, or avoiding altogether the problems that are now most pressing."[12]

The DGND studio sequence flows from this premise and, coupled with the luxury of a three-year commitment to teaching an advanced, interdisciplinary studio from the University of Pennsylvania, allowed me to map out a linked, multi-year process around questions of how to make the field of landscape architecture more useful to the climate justice movement. The DGND studios were never intended to offer a quick or easy solution to the problems of design education under capitalism. Rather, their development emerged from a recognition that any pedagogy or praxis aimed at subverting capitalist hegemony within a design school must be organized around the idea that "before landscape problems can be *solved*, they must be *framed*. Solutionism short-circuits this crucial step."[13] They are linked by sites—including Appalachia, the Mississippi Delta, and the Corn Belt—and by a commitment to experiments with pedagogy, climate fiction storytelling, and a series of briefs that take the principles of the Green New Deal, the Red Deal, and the Red, Black, and Green New Deal as serious propositions for the future of the planet. Richard Weller joined the first iteration of this studio as a special adviser in 2019, the second iteration concluded in the fall of 2020, and a third in 2021.

These studios are framed around two key concepts: probing and usable speculation. Within each studio and across the entire series, the concept of probing is derived from Karen Lutsky and Sean Burkholder's "Curious Methods" essay. In it, they write that "probing is a mode of exploration that informs but does not limit. It is a creative process that involves asking and enacting questions…and is a non-linear operation…involving three components: inquiry, the process of asking and enacting questions; insight, which is generated through that process; and impression, or the representation of those activities."[14] Within each DGND studio, probing is structured into the work through a hybrid seminar-studio model of pedagogy. Over the first four to six weeks of each semester, students are engaged in close reading and discussion of critical historical, theoretical, and sociological texts tied to issues of climate justice,[15] the energy transition,[16] statecraft,[17] and particular places,[18] before any drawing, mapping, or design work begins.

As these seminars conclude, students then work in teams focused on a specific region (Appalachia, the Mississippi Delta, and the Corn Belt) to produce two key analytics products, informed by their seminar discussions: a manifesto, which serves both as a working conceptual framework for the students to begin understanding the sequence of extractive regimes that helped shape their region's political, economic, and cultural history and present *and* an argument for how and why to propose futures for them; and an atlas of the region, blending fieldwork (oral histories and interviews with local activists), counter-cartographies, and other spatial phenomena into a coherent package of images. These assignments are directly linked to Judith Schalansky's conceptual framework in *An Atlas of Remote Islands* that states "I didn't realize then that my atlas—like every other—was committed to an ideology. Its ideology was clear from its map of the world, carefully positioned on a double-page spread so that the Federal Republic of Germany and the German Democratic Republic fell on two separate pages…geographical maps are abstract and concrete at the same time; for all the objectivity of their measurements, they cannot represent reality, merely one interpretation of it."[19] Each of these assignments—the seminar, the manifesto, and the atlas—are tethered to the principles of inquiry, insight, and impression that comprise probing. This work forms the first half of each studio, with the manifesto and atlas forming the core of the mid-review.

For the rest of the semester, students are challenged to engage in what I've termed usable speculation. The modifier "usable" is doing significant work here. It draws on the concept of "usable pasts" from public historians, in which "past national experiences can be placed in the service of the future"[20] and that "we must learn how to make a better world out of usable pasts rather than dreaming of infinite futures."[21] This is distinct from most other forms of design fiction and speculation, which often align with the methods and principles in Anthony Dunne and Fiona Raby's *Speculative Everything*[22] – a delightful book that treats speculation as a mostly technological and aesthetic proposition, eliding the blinders of capitalist realism, the constraints of contemporary politics, and, crucially, the demands of movements. In each studio, core collaborators are brought into the work by the instructor—most of whom are longtime collaborators in other contexts—as new groups and individuals are identified. As each studio concludes, some of the work is often carried forward through ongoing, collaborative projects based in the McHarg Center and has included the Sunrise Movement, Gulf Coast Center for Law and Policy, the Green New Deal Network, and the Red, Black, and Green New Deal.

More instrumentally, the concept of usable speculation also engages with the theory of change that no one will ever understand or rally around an energy transition through molecules (carbon in the atmosphere) or electrons (electricity in their circuits). Rather, people will only understand it through material investments in their lives and livelihoods – through the buildings, commutes, offices, parks, public works, and civic infrastructure that stitch together everyday life. So, in coproducing cli-fi with leaders from the climate justice movement, these studios aim to both illustrate their demands and, in doing so, to advance them by giving form, aesthetic, and visual culture to their demands – reframing conversations about climate justice and the Green New Deal from one of scarcity (for example, a ban on airplanes and hamburgers) to one of dignity and plenty. Within this framework of usable speculation, students are then charged with proposing and developing their own storytelling vehicles – things that have ranged from graphic novels and zines, to cookbooks and farmer's almanacs, to children's books, among many others.

In these studios, design is viewed as an instrument of redistributive climate justice. Speculative design in particular is framed as a medium for translating the often-abstract demands of the various movements for justice into compelling, charismatic images and stories about the future worlds they intend to create. This isn't merely an exercise in illustration, but rather a way of testing those demands – by giving them form and aesthetic, and by landing them in real communities and on real sites, through storytelling that opens possibilities for the future rather than putting forward a singular, idealized future. Drawing on the work of Ruth Levitas in *Utopia as Method*[23] and others in similar veins, students are challenged to develop the imagery and iconography of the world that Green New Dealers intend to build – often rooted in the idea that the fight for a Green New Deal becomes at least a bit easier when the frame of conversation moves from one of scarcity to one of beautiful, communitarian, low-carbon luxury for all. In that spirit, the advisers and jurors for these studios are comprised primarily of frontline and fence-line activists; movement leaders at organizations like the Sunrise Movement, the Gulf Coast Center for Law and Policy, People's Action, and the Democratic Socialists of America; and academic designers with affinities for or real connections to one or more of these movements. Though this work is only the beginning, it is part of a larger project within the design professions – one that involves real political education within schools of design, materialist commitments to communities and issues throughout the professions, and a more confrontational role (at least within academia) with the systems of immiseration that shape design practice around the world. If the Green New Deal is about a total restructuring of the economy, then the DGND studios have been about finding a place for the design professions within that process.

1. Daniel Aldana Cohen, "Eco-Apartheid is Real," *The Nation* (July 26, 2019).

2. Billy Fleming, "Crises and Contestations: The Promise and Peril of Designing a Green New Deal," *Architectural Digest* (in press).

3. Naomi Klein, *This Changes Everything: Capitalism Versus the Climate* (Simon & Schuster Books, 2014), 172.

4. Olufemi Taiwo & Liam Kofi Bright, "A Response to Michael Waltzer," *Dissent Magazine* (August 7, 2020).

5. Nick Gill, et al., "Carceral Circuitry: New Directions in Carceral Geography," *Progress in Human Geography* 42, no. 2 (2018): 183–204.

6. Oliver Wainwright, "The despot dilemma: should architects work for repressive regimes?" *The Guardian* (January 27, 2020).

7. Peggy Deamer, *Architecture and Capitalism: 1845 to Present* (Routledge, 2014), 1–2.

8. Douglas Spencer, *The Architecture of Neoliberalism: How Contemporary Architecture Became an Instrument of Control and Compliance* (Bloomsbury, 2016), 4.

9. Mark Fisher, *Capitalist Realism: Is There No Alternative?* (Zero Books, 2009), 1–11.

10. For more on this, see Cedric Robinson, *Black Marxism: The Making of the Black Radical Tradition* (UNC Press, 1983); and Ruth Wilson Gilmore, *Golden Gulag: Prisons, Surplus, Crisis, and Opposition in Globalizing California* (University of California Press, 2007).

11. Reinhold Martin, *Knowledge Worlds: Media, Materiality, and the Making of the Modern University* (Columbia University Press, 2021).

12. Rob Holmes, "The Problem with Solutions," *Places Journal* (July 2020).

13. Ibid.

14. Karen Lutsky & Sean Burkholder, "Curious Methods," *Places Journal* (May 2017).

15. Readings included *US House Resolution 109*, "Recognizing the duty of the Federal Government to create a Green New Deal"; Kate Aronoff, et al., *A Planet to Win: Why We Need a Green New Deal* (Verso, 2019); and Kian Goh, "Planning the Green New Deal: Climate Justice and the Politics of Sites and

Scales," *Journal of the American Planning Association* 86, no. 2 (2020): 188–95.

16. Readings included Myles Lennon, "Decolonizing Energy: Black Lives Matter and technoscientific expertise amid solar transitions," *Energy & Social Science* 30 (2017): 18–27; Johanna Bozuwa, "The Case for Public Ownership of the Fossil Fuel Industry," *The Next System Project* (April 14, 2020); and Reinhold Martin, "Abolish Oil," *Places Journal* (June 2020).

17. Readings included Brent Cebul, et al., *Shaped by the State: Toward a New Political History of the Twentieth Century* (University of Chicago Press, 2018); Michael Katz, *The Undeserving Poor: America's Enduring Confrontation with Poverty* (Oxford University Press, 2013); and Shalanda Baker, "Anti-Resilience: A Roadmap for Transformational Justice within the Energy System," *Harvard Civil Rights–Civil Liberties Law Review* 54 (2019): 1–48.

18. Readings included Clyde Woods, *Development Arrested: The Blues and Plantation Power in Mississippi* (Verso, 1998); Richard Mizelle, *Backwater Blues: The Mississippi Flood of 1927 in the African American Imagination* (University of Minnesota Press, 2014); Manu Karuka, *Empire's Tracks: Indigenous Nations, Chinese Workers, and the Transcontinental Railroad* (University of California Press, 2019); and Karida Brown, *Gone Home: Race and Roots through Appalachia* (University of North Carolina Press, 2018).

19. Judith Schalansky, *An Atlas of Remote Islands: Fifty Islands I Have Never Set Foot On and Never Will* (Penguin Books, 2009).

20. Van Wyck Brooks, "On Creating a Usable Past," *The Dial* 64, no. 7 (April 11, 1918): 337–41.

21. Tony Judt, "The Last Interview," *The Prospect* 173 (July 21, 2010).

22. Anthony Dunne & Fiona Raby, *Speculative Everything: Design, Fiction, and Social Dreaming* (The MIT Press, 2013).

23. Ruth Levitas, *Utopia as Method: The Imaginary Reconstitution of Society* (Palgrave, 2013).

AESTHETICS

James Andrew Billingsley

James Andrew Billingsley holds master's degrees in architecture and landscape architecture from the University of Pennsylvania and a bachelor's degree in geography from the University of Chicago. He has taught landscape architectural theory and technique at the University of Pennsylvania Weitzman School of Design and the University of Tennessee.

I n our epoch of disaster, it can be hard not to envy the strange people who inhabit the world of landscape architectural renderings. It is a happier world than ours. Bathed in the golden light of the Holocene, these stock figures enjoy a healthy lifestyle of bourgeois recreation. They cycle, jog, or stroll hand-in-hand, sometimes stopping to photograph flowers; or they lounge on clean white seatwalls or emerald lawns. The children dance with delirious abandon, releasing balloons or crouching to commune with fish and frogs. They appear to have solved the problems of pollution and urban sprawl; they worry little about forest fires or coastal flooding, if they have even heard of such things. They are happy to be in nature.

It makes sense that landscape architects choose to trade in images of an untroubled future – after all, our patrons depend on growth and optimism for their profits. For similar reasons, our profession tends to speak in terms of solutions. In addition to imagery, this bravado is evidenced in declarations, mission statements, profiles, trade rags, and "about" pages. I am of course not the first to observe landscape architecture's professional entanglement with neoliberalism and its enforced optimism, or to suggest that our ethics are compromised because of it. Instead, I propose a narrower question, simply about the operation of this landscape project. Does our work make any sense at all to people for whom nature is a source of sadness? In this essay I consider the consequences of a landscape architecture that engages with emotions more complex than the simple Arcadian bliss that has served as our foundation for centuries.

It is hard to perpetuate a fiction if you don't believe it yourself. While geologists and critics have continued to debate golden spikes and varieties of pithy "-cenes," the most revolutionary transformation of the Anthropocene—the mass extinction of meaning triggered by the death of nature—has already come to pass. Throughout the familiar centuries of the Holocene, nature could stand for creative freedom or oppressive fear, primal chaos or divine order, rational mechanism or transcendent indeterminacy, spiritual fellowship or dualistic hierarchy, bloody competition or holistic interobjectivity, whereas, in our era of anthropogenic apocalypse, nature first signifies its own disappearance. A rhino makes us think of its extinction, a glacier of its melting, a reef of its skeleton, a forest of its burning, and so on.

Landscape architecture is currently experiencing this epistemological apocalypse as a generational gap. Unlike most professors and partners, today's students and junior designers grew up in a world where IUCN extinction statistics and CO_2 concentrations were the stuff of children's magazines and grade-school science classes, and humanity's decision to surrender to carbon was a *fait accompli*. It is one thing to understand the world as something we are losing (that is, as something to fight to save) and quite another to believe that it was lost before we ever came on the scene – that the apocalypse is simply our inheritance. For the Anthropocene natives who have known no other world than this (and no other future), it is hard not to feel that quite a lot of the work we do—the blithe landscape-lands we draw for our clients—is bullshit.

A recent polemic by Billy Fleming positions contemporary landscape architecture within the larger project of neoliberalism, understood through the lens of the late philosopher Mark Fisher's theory of "capitalist realism" – commonly glossed by Frederic Jameson's aphorism that it is more difficult to imagine the end of the world than the end of capitalism. Fleming's productive response is an alternative model of studio education, opposed to corporate practice and its grinding foundation in the ritualized debasement of design students. This pedagogy offers a speculative view through to the other side of Fisher's aphorism: that is, it proposes to help us imagine a post-capitalist world, by developing imagery and iconography for the future that Green New Dealers hope to build, "of beautiful, communitarian, low-carbon luxury for all."[1]

Progressive alternative models like Fleming's are vital to our discipline's chances of having any relevance to humanity's future, beyond scattershot sustainabilizing of 22nd-century seafloors. But the unfortunate truth is that no matter how hard we work, there are many futures in which the Green New Deal never comes to pass, in which every success is matched by two tragedies, in which nature remains a source of sadness. It is not defeatism to consider such outcomes. Rather, ignoring them is a dereliction of our responsibility to consider the reception of our designs, whether they exist in a utopia or in a permanently tarnished world. The Anthropocene transition has a way of unsettling things as it smolders on; and in the face of unending disasters, we might take a second look at Jameson's aphorism. What if it is not the end of capitalism that we cannot imagine, but the end of the world itself? Or worse, what if the world has *already ended* but we just can't admit it? To borrow a question from the pessimism scholar Joshua Dienstag: "Who is it, exactly, that cannot bear a story unless guaranteed a happy ending?"[2]

But we remain equipped only to tell happy stories, whether in the service of capital or utopia. The problem is that while our mastery of performance and process has reached the level of science fiction, our aesthetic tools—how we actually engage *people*—are those of the 18th century. If Leon Battista Alberti was transported through time and deposited atop the Burj Khalifa or in the lobby of the Louis Vuitton Foundation, we might expect him to be at least somewhat disoriented by the strangeness of the architecture; but would Humphrey Repton really feel that out of place in any contemporary public park – no matter how much performance was crammed beneath his feet, or how parametric the benches?

It is not simply that the zombie picturesque is out-of-date or boring compared to the wizardry of modern architecture, but that this meta-style, which still dictates the public landscape of every city on earth, carries with it all the colonial oppression, class hierarchies, gender structures, racial erasure, and debunked proto-ecological precepts of its conception. While the death grip of the picturesque lingers on, our landscapes will continue to promulgate its fundamental axiom – that nature is a virtuous stage for human actors, unchanging and welcoming. And since our burning world reminds us every day that this axiom is false, then the primary effect of our anachronistic designs will be to spread cognitive dissonance, sadness, and melancholy – the psychological paralysis that comes from an inability to admit that the dead love object has truly died.[3]

The cure for melancholia is mourning. But as long as our landscapes condition humanity to cling to the Holocene, we will never be able to mourn the world we have lost; and we will remain stuck in the past, unable to move on to whatever world comes next. Landscape architects should be leaders in helping humans cope with life after the apocalypse, but in fact we are complicit in perpetuating the fiction that everything will be fine. It is not a coincidence that the popular medium most reminiscent of landscape architectural imagery is probably antidepressant commercials (although drug ads at least mention their side effects).

There is a great taboo among landscape architects against discussing the apocalypse on its own terms. Such talk is routinely written off as "doom and gloom," clichéd, unproductive – why waste your breath on doomsday if we'll all be gone anyway? But there are other kinds of apocalypses than the Western, biblical, Hollywood version (roll credits, see you in hell). Numberless people throughout history have seen their world end and continued living in the unfamiliar aftermath – challenged to make sense of the future as much as to survive in it. Julian Brave NoiseCat speaks of one North American nation's preservation of meaning through the catastrophe of colonialism: "If the Haudenosaunee can maintain their Great Law against an apocalypse, against genocide, I do believe that culture, and the stories that we tell about ourselves, and the words that we use to tell these stories, are some of the most powerful things that we have, to steel our souls against the climate abyss that we face now."[4]

If the poorly defined discipline of landscape architecture agrees on anything (at least since the Declaration of Concern), it is that "a sense of crisis has brought us together." We have the capacity to do a great many things: since the disasters of our era are linked through space, there are almost no challenges to which we cannot contribute. But if there is one thing that *only* we can do—the elusive "core knowledge"[5] of the discipline—it is reseeding the landscape with meaning following the epistemological apocalypse, the reduction of the natural world to a source of sadness. The project of landscape architecture after the Holocene is to help humanity understand how to exist in a post-apocalyptic world and, by acknowledging the poignancy of what has been lost, to enter the strange Anthropocene with some agency as a species.

If the tools we need for this project are primarily aesthetic, then we need new tools – Holocene thinking can't help us where we're going. I propose here three potential directions for investigating an authentic Anthropocene landscape aesthetic. Others remain to be discovered by the rising generation of Anthropocene-native designers who will, in the fraught years to come, determine the bounds of the discipline for themselves.

Permeable Boundaries

If the core operation of the picturesque is the reduction of nature to a passive, moralizing frame for human actors, then its successor must organize the world and its characters in a different way. We would be hard-pressed to envisage a less picturesque worldview than the wriggling universe of the object-oriented ontology (OOO) philosophers, who elevate rocks and bugs to the same existential status as humans, and who find inexhaustible profundity in the most commonplace of things. And while the architects who made first contact quickly forsook OOO's radical ecological promise for a crudely antinomian formalism, it always made more sense as landscape discourse anyway; the OOO evangelist Timothy Morton has asserted that "all architecture is landscape architecture," and we are clearly more comfortable working at the grand temporal and spatial scales of the hyperobject.[6]

OOO has much to offer landscape architecture; its injunction against reducing objects to simply what they *do* is a bracing corrective to our current monomaniacal focus on performance, and its exaltation of matter has proven seductive to designers eager to step back from systems theory and consider humbler things – flowers and concrete, animals and trash. But the thorny question of how to derive any semblance of a design methodology remains unanswered. As the OOO-architects proved, the simplistic idea that we should just design weirder-looking stuff is a creative and theoretical dead end.

One possible route forward is to shift our focus from the objects themselves to their outer boundaries – that is, the realm of aesthetic encounter. You and I will never know what it is like to be a rock or a spore; but we might be allowed gentle glances into their alien world, caught in the haze of analogy and affective response. Indeed, Timothy Morton himself charged Anthropocene designers in a foundational early essay with "establishing bonds of intimacy between beings."[7] A design ethic centered on mediating between different objects by modulating their porous boundaries constitutes a rebuke of the inviolate enclosedness of the human actor on a picturesque stage; and it accounts for the general leakiness of human civilization in the Anthropocene, in which nonhuman objects intrude into our bodies just as surely as our indiscriminate hand touches everything on the planet.

This mediative approach also resolves an obstacle facing the broader movement toward post-humanist landscape architecture. Research studios and experimental seminars continue to struggle to break the tautological circle of anthropocentrism – because, in the end, the agency and responsibility for intervention in the world still lies with the human designer. This is the correlationist trap identified by the speculative realists, but all the more pernicious because unlike philosophers, landscape architects eventually have to make things. We can guess at what sorts of landscapes nonhumans might enjoy living in, but this kind of affective roleplaying becomes pretty difficult when you move from orangutans to foxes to carp to mushrooms to flowers, let alone to rocks or gusts of wind.

In contrast, a methodology focused on mediating the aesthetic boundaries between objects ("establishing bonds of intimacy") acknowledges the agency of nonhumans without being afraid to admit that humans, in the end, need to design for humans. It is no longer possible, as it may have been in the Holocene, to separate humans from the nature they've created. We can't block out hyperobjects, which penetrate us from within just as much as they envelop us from without. But Anthropocene landscapes of interobjective permeability might just help humans come to grips with the fundamental strangeness of our new world without going insane.

Nonhuman Intelligences

In his recent taxonomy of currents in landscape architecture, Richard Weller identified 11 broad genres of creative ferment, from "resilience" to "iconoclasm." Only one of these 11, "digital natures,"[8] referenced the use of computational technology for landscape design; and the scope of computation was limited to the realm of sediment modeling. Some critics have designated the adoption of fluid modeling and parametric form-making as a "digital turn" in landscape architecture, paralleling the analogous moment in 1990s architecture; but this analogy only works if we reduce that period of wild aesthetic experimentation to simple mastery of performance and function.[9] Computational design is simply too transformative to be relegated to fluvial modeling and cyberpunk representation only vaguely correlated to actual design proposition.

Consider AI. Though skepticism of Silicon Valley is richly warranted, ignoring machine learning will simply ensure that its transformative potential will be left to malign actors and crude accelerationists. Alternative frameworks exist. The manifesto of the Indigenous Protocol and Artificial Intelligence Working Group deploys a Lakota word, wakȟáŋ, "that which cannot be understood…a fundamental principle in Lakota ontology's extension of interiority to a 'collective and universal' non-human." The authors ask: "Do the machines contain spirits already, given by an outside force?"[10] That is, only through the lens of Western anthropocentrism does it make sense to segregate AI from other nonhuman entities. In a flatter ontology, the thinking machine is just one more strange neighbor – not a unique signifier of human hubris.

Invoking AI as a mysterious nonhuman actor, summoned in a sort of Mephistophelian collaboration, offers another escape from the correlationist trap. For one thing, it's easier to bring AI into the studio than plants and animals. The welcoming of computer intelligences as a full partner in the development of de-anthropocentric landscapes, potentially mediated through the use of game engines (which designers are already becoming more familiar with) and techniques from the discipline of Human-Computer Interaction, promises to uncover novel digital landscape aesthetics, moving past the simplistic use of "datascapes" to improve the function of essentially picturesque landscape projects. This is fallow ground for our discipline. Even the speculative design ethos, which stands relatively alone in purporting to experiment with future landscapes, is much less concerned with authentic technological innovation than with the appearance of such (and with political revolution even less); and community-focused design tends to be syllogized with "low-tech," even as access to computation becomes wider with every passing year.

The key to an authentically Anthropocene computational landscape aesthetic is in demolishing these internal segregations and allowing the high-tech to cross-pollinate with the vegetal, the artistic, and the politically radical. This synthetic impulse might explain the rising interest in the writings of the political philosopher Jane Bennett, who offers a rare bridge between the delirious, if solipsistic, optimism of the posthumanists and new materialists and the real-life human struggle against oppressive systems. Of course, Bennett's vibrant materialism offers no more specific direction for designers than OOO. First steps toward operationalization exist; Rachel Armstrong's *Vibrant Venice* project stands out for its rigorous translation of ontology into methodology.[11] But it remains to be seen how these hybrid material practices can move from the gallery into the real world.

Landscape Existentialism

For a few hours in early June 2020, Philadelphians found themselves under three simultaneous lockdowns. There was the COVID-19 quarantine order (we were still afraid of outdoor transmission); there was a police curfew, covering Center City, decreed in response to the George Floyd protests that had exploded into existence on May 30; and, bizarrely, there was a tornado warning. Three crises at fever pitch—the pandemic, white supremacy, the climate—and in each case the state's response was to tell people to go home and shut their doors. What knots these strands together is their insistence that our public landscapes are places of life and death, despite the best efforts of their designers to hide the fact. What if our landscapes acknowledged trauma instead of repressing it?

Elaine Scarry writes that "when one hears about another person's physical pain, the events happening within the interior of that person's body may seem to have the remote character of some deep subterranean fact, belonging to an invisible geography that, however portentous, has no reality because it has not yet manifested itself on the visible surface of the earth.'"[12] There is pain in abundance in our time of Anthropocene transition. An intentionally post-apocalyptic landscape architecture must seek to make this pain legible, from one object to another, human and nonhuman. This is the opposite of the picturesque, which has always been a tool for masking conflict, whether between groups of people or between people and the world itself.

We are well equipped, as the only designers whose media live and die, to meet the Anthropocene's existential challenges on existential grounds. Existentialism can free us from blithe problem-solving; after all, the graveyard remains the only brief that allows us to engage with emotions other than delight or preachy ecological moralizing (despite ongoing efforts to rebrand cemeteries as multi-performative fitness-scapes, the public still stubbornly insists on feeling sad at funerals). In *Black Landscapes Matter*, Walter Hood describes the dialectical power of uncovering trauma, even as white hegemony pathologically erases and denatures Black landscapes and history; yet it is precisely this neglect that allows the process of rediscovery to become radically generative. "The contested and the forgotten landscapes, renewed through a myriad of expressions, can give us incentives to obligations for years to come…The period of neglect can be seen as a powerful 'pregnant pause.' It can be a time to develop new concepts of history without being thwarted by the old, which must die and be rejected."[13]

It is worth considering that perhaps the most iconic landscape intervention of our moment of crisis is not high-tech, not green infrastructure, not performative; it is the monumental yellow-on-black logoscape of Black Lives Matter Plaza, inscribed in Washington DC and cities worldwide as a dialectical product of 2020's uprisings. A city street transformed into an unambiguous statement about the value of human life, in words legible from outer space – an existential landscape, literally. The deathless Arcadia that our landscapes all still reference is irrelevant in our epoch of unrest; it simply remains for our discipline to admit it.

The truth is that aesthetic movements cannot be predicted or prescribed beforehand. Whatever emerges to replace the archaic virtue of the late-Holocene picturesque will be a spontaneous collaboration between many designers in every part of the earth. The three strands proposed here are potential directions for exploration. Not every direction of practice will be object-oriented, computational, or existentialist. Our overlapping crises condition a multitude of critiques, from all the diversity that our world provides. But they are all rooted in the central trauma of the Anthropocene transition: the pain of having experienced the end of the world.

And the responsibility for helping humanity process this trauma is one that we cannot abdicate. Reflecting on the failure of artists to engage the bloody human disasters of the 1990s and 2000s—Srebrenica, Rwanda, the World Trade Center—the architect Lebbeus Woods asked:

> If we concede the impotence of plastic art in interpreting horrific evens so close to the core of modern existence, we in effect say goodbye to them as vital instruments of human understanding…Time itself has collapsed. The need is urgent. Can art help us here in the white heat of human struggle for the human, or must we surrender our hope for comprehension to the political and commercial interests that have never trusted art?… People need works of art to mediate between themselves and the often incomprehensible conditions they live with…What are the authentic forms of interpreting ruins—the death of the human, indeed, ultimately, of everything—today?[14]

He wasn't writing about the climate apocalypse, but he might as well have been. Landscape architecture has fought valiantly to forestall the end of the world, and it is a legacy we should be proud of; but it is time to address ourselves to the question of how people will live in the world yet to come.

1. Billy Fleming, "Frames and Fictions: Designing a Green New Deal Studio Sequence," *Journal of Architectural Education*, 75, no. 2 (2021): 200.

2. Joshua Foa Dienstag, *Pessimism: Philosophy, Ethic, Spirit* (Princeton University Press), x.

3. Sigmund Freud, "Trauer und Melancholie [Mourning and Melancholia]," *Internationale Zeitschrift für Ärztliche Psychoanalyse [International Journal for Medical Psychoanalysis]* (1917).

4. Julian Brave NoiseCat, keynote discussion, "Designing a Green New Deal" conference, held at the University of Pennsylvania Ian L. McHarg Center for Urbanism and Ecology, Philadelphia (September 13, 2019).

5. Anne Whiston Spirn, "Ian McHarg, Landscape Architecture, and Environmentalism: Ideas and Methods in Context," *Environmentalism in Landscape Architecture* 22 (2000): 100.

6. Timothy Morton, lecture, "The Golden Stain of Time," SCI-Arc (March 7, 2017).

7. Timothy Morton, "Architecture Without Nature," *tarp: Architecture Manual* 10 (2012): 3.

8. Richard Weller, "Landscape Genres: Towards a taxonomy of landscape architecture in the 21st century," *Landscape Architecture Frontiers* 26, no. 8 (July 2019): 168.

9. See, for example, Jillian Walliss, "Landscape Architecture and the Digital Turn: Towards a productive critique," *JoLA* 13, no. 3 (2018).

10. Jason E. Lewis, et al., "Making Kin with the Machines," *Journal of Design and Science* (July 16, 2018).

11. Rachel Armstrong, *Vibrant Architecture: Matter as a codesigner of living structures* (De Gruyter Open, 2015).

12. Elaine Scarry, *The Body in Pain: The making and unmaking of the world* (Oxford University Press, 1985), 3.

13. Walter Hood, *Black Landscapes Matter* (University of Virginia Press, 2020), 4.

14. Lebbeus Woods, "Doom Time," lebbeuswoods.blogspot.com (June 8, 2009).

AFTERWORD

At the beginning of the third decade of the 21st century the shock of climate change and the advent of the Anthropocene are now sinking in as realities. Scientists are redoubling their efforts to understand how the earth—including human activity—works as a whole, and humanists are deconstructing the conceptual foundations of modernity and reassembling the philosophical, ethical, and political scaffolding around which a more ecological and equitable future could grow. The project of landscape architecture—as is implied by its very name—is to bring these sciences and humanities together in the act of designing places. At the same time, other professions involved in the constructed environment are increasingly looking to landscape as a medium through which stronger resilience and identity can be achieved. Without self-serving histrionics, it is fair to say that landscape architecture finds itself in a significant and timely position.

However, whether landscape architecture can rise to the occasion is by no means a given. The profession is still extremely vulnerable to marginalization by its older siblings and despite the global phenomenon of environmentalism, the medium of landscape itself is still subject to trivialization in popular culture. For its part, as it seeks to expand the discipline's purview, landscape architecture's small yet aspirational academy risks overreaching and losing itself in any number of fashionable, transdisciplinary forays. To an extent this is as it should be—the whole planet is, after all, landscape—but to enter into fruitful collaborations the discipline, and by extension the profession, needs a strong core, and this core comes from design. In an especially holistic manner, design is the one thing the landscape architect can bring to the table that others cannot. And in a world where every stone has by now been turned over and everything is competing for space, the design of the land is a necessity, not a luxury.

The critic might interject here that there appears to be no design in this book. It is certainly true that we decided not to do (yet another) lavish book of designs, but rather a book about design; in particular, about what landscape architectural design might yet become. Consequently, with only occasional exception where needed to support an argument, the authors were asked not to use this publication to showcase their own practices. These are well documented elsewhere. The brief was to begin with a certain rubric—agriculture, water, plants, etcetera—and, with this as a lens, speak to the future of the field. Each essay attempts, then, to conjoin the particular to the general and each can stand alone; but the bigger idea here is that the holistic and ambitious nature of what is meant by the landscape project only comes into full focus when all the essays are collaged together.

Not to put too fine a point on it – the landscape project is now a matter of survival for human and nonhuman alike. But unlike other species that shuffled headlong into their own extinction, humanity is at least aware of its self-induced ecological predicament. For those with the privilege to broach problems as creative challenges, this awareness translates into the foresight of design. This failing world didn't just happen, it was designed; and now it has to be undesigned and redesigned. Thinking of history this way we are not at the beginning of the end, we are at the beginning of an ecological design revolution. This revolution is not just about the usual pieties of bourgeoise altruism, as if things will be more or less the same only a bit greener, it is now a question of how a species is taking it upon itself to design an entire planet. It is about how all the artifacts of culture come from and return to that planet, and how they perform in between.

For landscape architects, Le Corbusier's provocation "architecture or revolution" was replaced in 1969 by Ian McHarg's "design with nature." Both oversimplified the world and dangerously reduced design to instrumentality, but because the latter works from the ground up instead of the bird's-eye view down, it has proven the more prescient. For revolutionaries, of course, both are no good: architecture is egotistical and oppressive; nature is apolitical and romantic; and even if it were more ethical and more powerful, design is too slow for the ensuing chaos of the climate crisis. Yes and no. History teaches that the alternative to design—violent revolution—exciting and necessary as it may seem, is likely to backfire. So too, the clarity and simplicity of any utopia (today's socialist ecotopias included) always contain the seeds of their own dystopia.

The foresight of design, without a naïve belief in technofixes, is all we have. In addition to language, it's all humans have ever really had. The redesign of modern objects, systems, and settlements—the relics of a fossil-fueled world—will happen, but it will not be easy and it will not be fast. And although in that time there will be horrendous loss, there is reason for optimism in a climate-changed world. As the world urbanizes and global population declines, and as the energy transition to renewables simultaneously builds, the anthropogenic pressure on the earth system will lessen. Add to this the possibility that through the climate crisis humanity will not just be reminded of its hubris, but it will be profoundly humbled, then the physical and metaphysical prerequisites for us to enter into a more symbiotic and less parasitic relationship with the earth will be established.

In the interim, design has to work at absorbing the shock, creating refugia, limiting the suffering, and, wherever possible, bringing joy in being mortally of the earth. Every landscape project, no matter how small, is a part of this "bigger picture." Philosophically and practically, this means not just designing with nature—as if it is still some other thing—but designing within nature: learning its codes and working within its strict evolutionary limits, but at the same time finding novelty within its fundamentally creative propensity for life.

Richard J. Weller and Tatum L. Hands

NOTES